THE WAR
& THE PROPHETS

NOTES ON CERTAIN POPULAR PREDICTIONS
CURRENT IN THIS LATTER AGE

BY

HERBERT THURSTON, S.J.

Μάντις ἄριστος ὅστις εἰκάζει καλῶς

St. Pius X Press Inc.
Copyright 2012
ISBN: 1480016470
www.stpiusxpress.com

PREFACE

THIS little book, dealing with the prophecies current during or recalled to memory by the present war, has been suggested at least in part by Döllinger's well-known essay, *Der Weissagungsglaube und das Prophetenthum in der christlichen Zeit,* of which an excellent translation was published forty years ago by Mr. Alfred Plummer. Dr. Döllinger's survey dealt almost exclusively with the predictions of the Middle Ages; the present work concerns itself with those prognostics which have attracted attention in recent times, and are expected to find their fulfilment in our own generation. Even Döllinger, in spite of his strongly antipapal standpoint, did not think of questioning the possibility of a genuine gift of prophecy, whether natural or infused. He believed, for example, that Savonarola possessed it, although by no means all Savonarola's predictions were justified by the sequel. Naturally it is not the aim of the following pages to show that credibility is to be denied on principle to every attempt to foretell future events. St. Paul writes, as we all know :

Preface

"Despise not prophecies, but prove all things, hold fast that which is good" (1 Thess. v. 20-21); and although, as Lightfoot well notes, the meaning of προφητεία in the New Testament is "forth-telling rather than foretelling," inspiration, in other words, rather than prediction, still the latter sense is also implicitly included. That there have been, and are, many persons to whom a knowledge of the future is imparted in ways that transcend our comprehension, I fully believe. But that this knowledge ever extends to the foreseeing of political events of general interest is very difficult to establish by evidence. It does not seem to be part of the divine dispensation that assurance regarding the decrees of Providence should be given to any considerable body of mankind. Certainly a careful scrutiny of such pretended oracles as are discussed in the present volume must lead to an attitude of extreme suspicion in regard to all literature of this type. Of the many hundred predictions recorded in the various collections which I have examined almost all have been long ago refuted by the actual course of events. I have, in fact, come across but one, and that a prophecy to which attention has not hitherto been directed, which seems to me to retain the least semblance of intrinsic probability (see pp. 80-84 below). Moreover, even here the extrinsic evidence is quite unsatisfactory, and should the terrible catastrophe foreshadowed unhappily come anywhere near realization, one

Preface

could feel no confidence that we were in the presence of anything more than a rather exceptional coincidence.

Although the longest chapter in this volume, that concerned with the pretended " prophecy of St. Malachy," may seem at first sight to have little to do with the present war, the observant reader will soon discover that these papal mottoes are closely interwoven with the fabric of nearly all the recent religious predictions concerning present calamities and the end of the world. It therefore seemed desirable to discuss the question of the fraudulent origin of the list in some detail, the more so that much that is written on the subject is curiously ill-informed. The substance of the chapter dealing with St. Malachy is taken from two articles which I contributed to *The Month* as far back as June and July, 1899, where the intimate dependence of the mottoes on Panvinio was, I think, made clear for the first time. The fact that even in such a work as *The Catholic Encyclopædia* the " prophecy " should be treated as a document of serious value seemed to render it needful to deal with the subject somewhat more fully and exhaustively than the matter in itself deserved.

March 31st, 1915.

CONTENTS

CHAPTER I

PROPHECY IN 1870-1   1

CREDULITY at seasons of popular excitement—The war of 1870—Vogue of the *Voix Prophétiques* and of other similar collections—Blessed Catherine of Racconigi—Anna Maria Taigi and the three days of darkness—Madeleine Poisat and Maximin of La Salette—The famous prophecy of Orval—Henry V, the "Offspring of the Cap"—A suggested alliance for Queen Victoria—The Orval prophecy an avowed forgery—The failure of Mary Lataste—The prophecy of Blois—King George's "isle of captivity."

CHAPTER II

THE PROPHETS AND ECCLESIASTICAL AUTHORITY   26

PROTESTS of Father de Buck and Mgr. Dupanloup—The fifth Council of Lateran—Mgr. Douais—The Question of Imprimaturs—The Saint of Toulouse—Supposed Prophecy of the Curé D'Ars; its real meaning—Unsatisfactoriness of the evidence—The "Feast of our Lady" an interpolation—The Dom Bosco fabrication.

CHAPTER III

"BROTHER JOHANNES"   47

TEXT of the Prophecy—The Antichrist—The Battle of the Beasts—Incredible profusion of detail—Sar Péladan and his extravagances—A free-and-easy editor—Madame Faust and M. Péladan's recitation—The strange omissions of Brother Johannes—Prediction attributed to St. Thomas of Canterbury—Other Beast prophecies.

Contents

CHAPTER IV

ARMAGEDDON AND THE END OF WAR ... ... PAGE 68

THE Battle of the Birch Tree—Jaspers—The bogus Prophecy of Mayence—Hermann of Lehnin—The Polish vision of Blessed Andrew Bobola—The predictions of a modern Carmelite nun —" 'Till only the fourth part of men remain "— Flaws in the evidence—A letter to an English priest.

CHAPTER V

DIVINERS AND SOOTHSAYERS 90

AN arithmetical prognostic of the year of the Kaiser's downfall—Such cabbalistic divinations no novelty—Louis Napoleon's fatal year—An illustration from the eighteenth century—The numerical significance of *Pius papa nonus*—The methods of Zadkiel and Old Moore—" Men marke when they hit and never marke when they misse "—Some modern horoscopes—The commercial value of a gift of reading the stars—Madame de Thèbes—Nostradamus—A Mother Shipton fabrication—The death of a sovereign correctly foretold.

CHAPTER VI

THE SO-CALLED " PROPHECY OF ST. MALACHY " 120

VOGUE of St. Malachy's papal mottoes—How first published—Triviality and purposeless character of the interpretations—Fundamental difference between the mottoes which precede and those which follow the date of publication—Vagueness and ready adaptability of the later oracles—The Pope book of Panvinio—This book unquestionably used for the fabrication of the mottoes—Overwhelming evidence which proves this assertion—Panvinio's blunders of 1557 incorporated in St. Malachy's supposed prophecy of 1142—Origin of the forgery—Theories of Weingarten and Harnack—Grounds for rejecting them—The Popes still to come and the inferences drawn from their mottoes.

Contents

CHAPTER VII

THE FATE OF ENGLAND AND THE COMING OF ANTICHRIST 142

NATIONAL prophecies—Nostradamus predicts 300 years of maritime empire for England—An English revolution also foretold—Mlle. Couédon—Bartholomew Holzhauser and England's reconversion to the Faith—Prophecy of St. Edward the Confessor—Antichrist according to the *Ascension of Isaiah*—Adso's great Emperor of Frankish race—Roger Bacon's *Papa Angelicus*—The two ideas combined in the later mediæval legends—St. Vincent Ferrer on the near approach of the end of the world—Antichrist already born—St. Francis of Paolo's supposed prophecy—Holzhauser and many other mystics predict for the Church a period of peace and triumph which is to precede Antichrist—Conflicting views regarding the date and order of the events which herald the second coming of Christ.

THE WAR AND THE PROPHETS

CHAPTER I

PROPHECY IN 1870—1871

EVERY schoolboy is familiar with the portents which in the pages of Livy are noted as occurring in profusion at seasons of special danger and calamity in the history of the republic. But even Livy, respecter of traditions as he was, did not disguise his misgivings regarding the authenticity of many of the preternatural occurrences which he thought it incumbent upon him to record. Thus it is that at a breathing space in his chronicle of the second Punic war he remarks: "At Rome or in the neighbourhood many portents occurred that winter, or, as often happens when once men's minds are affected by religious fears, many were reported and thoughtlessly believed."[1] There can in any case be no

---

[1] Livy, Lib. xxi, cap. 62. "Romæ aut circa urbem multa ea hieme prodigia facta, aut, quod evenire solet motis semel in religionem animis, multa nuntiata et temere credita sunt." *Cf.* xxii 1 and 36; xxiii 32; xxiv 10 and 44, etc.

doubt that an atmosphere of excitement and unrest is singularly favourable for the propagation of credulities of all kinds.[1] We need not exactly call it nerves, that is, if nerves be supposed to be synonymous with a condition of abject terror. There is often no terror; terror in fact is the effect rather than the cause. But there is a loss of mental balance, a disposition to clutch at straws, an inability to observe any outward object without magnifying it tenfold, and we must believe that this attitude of mind is distinctly unhealthy. It may at times be a stimulus, but a stimulus which is followed by a regrettable reaction. The more we can maintain an attitude of robust common sense the better for ourselves and for our neighbours. Our British phlegm, which is not perhaps nowadays quite so distinctively British a characteristic as it used to be, is a valuable asset at times such as these.

I am led to make these reflections by the indications which meet us on so many sides just now of a general disposition to credulity, not only with regard to statements of fact and horrors committed in the war, but also with regard to predictions concerning the future. At the time of the great Franco-Prussian contest of 1870—1871 there was a positive epidemic of pro-

[1] Döllinger, *Prophecies and the Prophetic Spirit*, Eng. trans., pp. 89-90, points out how rife prophecies were upon the disturbed soil of Italy, and also how they multiplied during the time of the Great Schism; *ib.*, p. 152.

"Voix Prophétiques"

phecies, especially on the French side. A certain Abbé Curicque, a member of various learned societies, compiled a work, which in its fifth edition, published in 1872, filled more than thirteen hundred pages with vaticinations supposed to refer to our present age.[1] Though a large proportion of these utterances profess to have emanated from canonized saints or from persons in repute of holiness, it would be impossible to find a single item which could have given a clue to any event known to have happened since the book was published, or which was even likely to be helpful, except in the most general way, to readers in search of moral edification. For the most part the predictions are obscure and hopelessly elusive. Notwithstanding their Christian origin they are not one whit more easy of interpretation than the oracles of pagan Delphi. If ever they seem to offer a definite indication of something capable of investigation, they either prove to have been

[1] *Voix Prophétiques, ou Signes, Apparitions et Prédictions Modernes touchant les grands événements de la Chrétienté au XIXe siècle et vers l'approche de la Fin des Temps*, par l'Abbé J. M. Curicque, Membre de la Société d'Archéologie et d'Histoire de la Moselle, etc., 5th ed., 2 vols., Paris: Palmé, 1872. A vast number of similar books appeared about the same time, *e.g.*, Père Marie Antoine, *Le Grand Pape et le Grand Roi*, 7th ed., Toulouse, 1872; V. de Stenay, *Le Prophète David Lazzeretti*, Paris, 1872; F. Roux, *Examen de la Prophétie de Blois*, Paris, 1871; Colin de Plancy, *La Fin des Temps*, Paris, 1871; V. de Stenay, *L'Avenir dévoilé*, Paris, 1870, 1871; A. Le Pelletier, *La Clef des Temps*; G. Naquet, *Europe Délivrée*, Paris, 1871; etc., but it would be useless to attempt a bibliography.

falsified by subsequent events, or when compared with one another, they lead us to contradictory conclusions. A more unprofitable task than that of the editor who with great labour gathered up these *Voix Prophétiques,* it would be impossible to imagine.

Without attempting to furnish any account of the heavenly portents with which the book is filled—the apparitions of saints, the moving statues, the testimony of possessed persons, the armies, crosses and serpents seen in the air, the menacing aspect of the *aurora borealis,* the shocks of earthquake, the dried-up fountains that began to flow, etc., etc.[1]—all of which are represented as full of prophetic significance, one or two brief illustrations may be given of utterances in which the prophet, or more probably the prophet's interpreters, have been sufficiently ill-advised to venture upon definite statements and dates. For the most part the works of canonized saints, for example, St. Bridget, St. Gertrude, St. Theresa, St. Leonard of Port Maurice, etc., which are laid under contribution, furnish no

[1] As a mere matter of curiosity it may be interesting to translate the headings of the chapters of Book V, they correspond to pp. 401-53 of vol. i (in the 4th ed.) and bear the general title " Prophetic Signs in the Elements." The chapters run as follows : 1, The Torrent of the Carceri of St. Francis of Assisi ; 2, The overflow of the Tiber ; 3, The intermittent spring of Darbres ; 4, The Aurora Borealis of Oct. 24th and 25th, 1870 ; 5, The cross of light around the moon on the night of December 8th ; 6, The monster serpent seen in the air at Jarny, near Metz ; 7, The battle in the sky at the village of Golaze in Poland ; 8, Three military scenes witnessed in the heavens by observers in the Rhineland ; 9, The earthquake in Tibet.

Anna Maria Taigi

more than general premonitions of calamity for the Church, which might belong to any age or any combination of circumstances. But some of the utterances of persons in repute of sanctity are represented as being more explicit. Thus we learn that Blessed Catherine of Racconigi announced, before 1544, that after three centuries had elapsed, a descendant of Francis I, King of France, should rule over the world like a second Charlemagne.[1] There is a little difficulty here, since the male line of Francis I came to an end with Henry III, but the editor thinks it obvious that the royal house of Bourbon in general must be meant, and the partisans of the Comte de Chambord were consequently left free to derive all encouragement from this prediction of a universal Christian monarchy. Unfortunately we have come to the end of almost four centuries since Blessed Catherine prophesied, and the advent of the second Charlemagne seems as far off as ever. The Venerable Anna Maria Taigi, according to the *Voix Prophétiques*, was much more precise. She announced that the pontificate of Pius IX would last twenty-seven years.[2] He was in fact Pope for nearly thirty-two years. Moreover, she very definitely asserted that he would live to see the triumph of the Church in spite of all the calamities that would previously come upon the world. Indeed we

[1] *Voix Prophétiques*, vol. ii, p. 100.
[2] *Voix*, ii, 167.

have quite a minute description of all the occurrences which would then take place:

All the enemies of the Church, hidden or open, will perish during the days of darkness with the exception of some few whom God will convert immediately afterwards.

The air will then be infected by the demons who will appear under all kinds of hideous shapes. The possession of a blessed candle will secure its owner from death, so also will the saying of prayers addressed to our Blessed Lady and the holy angels.

After the days of darkness, Saints Peter and Paul having come down from heaven, will preach throughout the world and will designate the new Pope, *Lumen in Coelo*,[1] who is to succeed Pius IX. A great light will flash from their bodies and will settle upon the cardinal, the future pontiff.

Saint Michael the Archangel, appearing then upon earth in human form, will hold the devil enchained until the period of the preaching of Antichrist.

In these days, Religion shall extend its empire throughout the world. There shall be " one Shepherd." The Russians will be converted, as well as England and China, and all the faithful will be filled with joy in beholding this overwhelming triumph of the Church.

After the days of darkness, the Holy House of Loreto will be carried by the angels to Rome and will be deposited in the basilica of Saint Mary Major.[2]

---

[1] This, of course, is a reference to the so-called prophecy of St. Malachy, which is discussed later on in chapter vi.

[2] *Voix Prophétiques* (5th ed., 1872), vol. ii, pp. 170-1. (3rd ed., 1871) pp. 342-3.

Madeleine Poisat

I am far from asserting, or even believing, that the Venerable Anna Maria Taigi was herself the author of this rubbish. But when the cause of her Beatification was being pressed forward at Rome, these things were attributed to her, and they do not seem to have been repudiated by those who were officially associated with the inquiry. Certain it is, in any case, that what I have just quoted appears in the third, fourth, and fifth editions of the *Voix*, and that this last was not only recommended by letters from Bishops, but published with the express approbation of ecclesiastical authority. It must, of course, be remembered that all this saw the light while the humiliation of France and the loss of the temporal power were yet recent, and when Pius IX had still six or seven years of life before him. The same reflection explains the tone of a document which the editor of *Les Voix* declares to have been submitted to the Fathers of the Vatican Council[1] as a revelation vouchsafed to a holy mystic named Madeleine Poisat. Here are a few sentences:

Peter have confidence. The ark outrides the storm and there follows a great calm. Pius IX is the last Pope of the Church oppressed, "Cross of the Cross" (*Crux de Cruce*).[2] Pain for him but also joy. After him comes deliverance. *Lumen in coelo* (Light in the heaven). It is the eye of Mary.

[1] *Voix*, ii, 476.
[2] Another reference to the Malachy prophecy.

Within the Church itself they will think that all is lost. Mary appears and lo! there is confusion, confusion even among priests.

And the seer goes on to explain that with the coming of Mary all will be converted, even the Jews and the Pharisees.

Of similar import is the so-called "secret" of Maximin Giraud, the shepherd boy, who, with Mélanie, was the witness of the apparitions of La Salette. The Editor of *Les Voix* professes to print from a copy made by the Venerable Pierre Eymard, the holy founder of the Society of the Blessed Sacrament, whose name is introduced as if he thus made himself guarantee for the authenticity of Maximin's pretended secret. Without quoting the whole we may note these events which will follow upon the loss of faith by three-quarters of the population of France:

A Protestant nation of the north will be converted to the faith, and by means of this nation the other nations will return to the faith.

The Pope who shall come after the present Pope, Pius IX, will not be Roman (*ne sera pas romain,* which might either mean that he would not be of Roman birth, or that he would have to establish his episcopal see elsewhere).

When men are converted God will restore peace to the world.

Afterwards this peace will be overthrown by the Beast (*le monstre*).

And the Beast will come at the end of the nineteenth century or at latest at the beginning of the twentieth.

So that we have apparently the conversion of England (?), the conversion of the world, a non-Roman pope, profound peace, and only after all these things, the coming of the Beast who is to upset the peace. None the less, the Beast is to arrive at latest at the beginning of the twentieth century!

Such were the prophecies which were widely circulated and greedily swallowed during the period of mental and political disturbance which followed upon the Franco-Prussian War. Needless to say that there were many which were understood to have a more direct reference to the final outcome of the drama which was then being enacted on the soil of France. Though Paris had capitulated before the end of January, 1871, some time had still to elapse before the treaty of peace was signed and a still longer period before the German garrisons, left behind to ensure the payment of the indemnity, were entirely withdrawn from French territory. This was of all others the season most fertile in prophecies of a forthcoming divine intervention. The Germans, it was believed, would manufacture some excuse for invading the country a second time. In punishment for the infidelities and crimes which had culminated in the horrors of the Commune, Paris would again become the prey of the enemy and would be almost entirely destroyed by fire. But when the humiliation of the French capital was complete, God would come to the aid of His faithful servants. A great leader would arise, whom every Legitimist identified with the Bourbon claimant, the Comte de Chambord. He would reign as king by the name of Henri V, and to the white standard which he unfurled all good Frenchmen would rally. The wicked would be exterminated, or else be converted, and the cause of Catholic Christianity would everywhere triumph. It was under the inspiration of ideas such as these that the prophecy attributed to the Curé d'Ars was disseminated in 1871-2. With this it will be necessary to deal more at length in a future chapter. In the meantime let me copy the latter portion of the much-debated " Prophecy of Orval," which more perhaps than any other augury gave encouragement to the supporters of Henri V.

The Prophecy of Orval was originally circulated as an ancient prediction which had been printed at Luxemburg in 1544. A copy of this booklet, it was said, chanced to be preserved in the neighbouring monastery of Orval (*Aurea Vallis*), and was thence made public in 1793. But others contented themselves with asserting more vaguely that, whatever its origin, the text was at least known to be in existence in the monastery before the French Revolution. The document, as we have it, begins with the rise of the great Napoleon and describes his career somewhat minutely. Seeing that the earliest printed copy dates only from 1839, this is not very convincing, neither is one more impressed by the fairly accurate presentment of the reigns of Louis XVIII and Charles X (1815-30), which almost certainly had already ended when the document first saw the light. The interest, of course, begins with what is obviously intended to be a forecast of the events after 1830; and here, as the unprejudiced reader will clearly discern, the prophet to all appearance knew nothing whatever of the Second Empire, but believed that after Louis Philippe[1] had reigned a few years he would be overthrown by another revolution. Then this new democracy, according to the forecast, would itself end in a period of terrible war and desolation, which would in turn be succeeded by the glorious rule of a legitimist monarch under whom the Church would triumph. Dates are not very clearly indicated, but the prophet seems to have believed that the Revolution, which he foresaw and which actually came in 1848, would last about ten years. After that he announced a purification by great calamities, which was to be followed by a sort of golden age in which a Bourbon king ("the offspring of the Cap," *i.e.*, a descendant of Hugh Capet) would bring prosperity both to France and to the Church. Apostrophizing, then, under the name of "Sons of Brutus," the Revolutionaries who were to depose Louis Philippe, the prophet goes on :

[1] He is clearly indicated under the phrase "Roi du Peuple."

22. Howl, ye sons of Brutus! Call upon the beasts that are going to devour you. Great God! what a clash of arms! A full number of moons is not yet completed, and behold, many warriors are seen coming!

23. The time is over. The desolated mountain of the Lord [the seven hills on which Rome is built] has cried unto God. The sons of Juda [the Bourbons; the kings of Israel were of the tribe of Juda] have cried to God from the foreign land, and behold, God is no longer deaf.

24. What a fire accompanies his arrows! Ten times six moons [five years] and again six times ten moons [five other years, or altogether ten years] have fed his anger.

25. Woe to thee great city! [presumably Paris]. Behold, there are many kings armed by the Lord, but fire has already levelled thee to the ground; yet the just will not perish, God has mercy upon them.

26. The abode of crime is purified by fire; the great river [the Seine] carries its waters all crimsoned with blood to the sea, and Gaul, nearly dismembered, will be reunited.

27. God loves peace. Come young Prince, quit the island of captivity. Listen; unite the lion and the white flower—come!

28. What is foreseen is the wish of God. The old blood of past centuries will again terminate long contentions, because then one sole pastor will be seen in Celtic-Gaul.

29. The man, powerful through God, will be firm on his throne, and many wise laws will establish peace. The offspring of the Cap will be so prudent and wise that God will be thought with him.

The Conversion of England 13

30. Thanks to the Father of mercies the Holy Sion proclaims again the glory of one great God.

31. Many lost sheep come and drink at the living stream; three kings and princes cast off the mantle of error [heresy] and see plainly the true faith of God.

32. At that time two third-parts of a great people of the sea [England and Scotland, Ireland being Catholic already] will return to the true faith.

33. God is again blessed during fourteen times six moons [seven years], and six times thirteen moons [about six years, or altogether thirteen years].

34. God is weary of having granted His mercies; nevertheless, for the sake of His elect He will prolong peace during ten times twelve moons [ten years].

35. God alone is great! All good is done; the saints are going to suffer. The man of evil arrives, born of two races.

36. The white flower becomes obscured during ten times six moons [five years], and six times twenty moons [ten years, or altogether fifteen years], and then disappears for ever!

37. Much evil and little good in those times; many cities perish by fire.

38. Then Israel comes to God Christ for good and all.

39. The accursed schismatics and the faithful people will be separated into two camps. But the time is over. God alone will be believed in, and the third part of Gaul, and again the third part and a half, will be without any creed.

40. It will be the same with other nations.

41. And behold, already six times three moons,

and four times five moons [altogether about three years] have passed since all things have been separated, and the last century has begun.

42. After a number not completed of moons, God combats through his two just ones, but the man of evil conquers. But all is over! The high God has placed a wall of fire before my understanding, and I can see no more.

We who now read this incoherent rhodomontade in cold blood find it difficult to restrain our impatience. It seems incredible that Frenchmen and Frenchwomen of intelligence can have pinned their faith to it as a supernatural revelation. And yet in France after the war there were literally scores of books written to vindicate its authenticity and to interpret its oracles as those of a sacred text.[1] Many pious writers took it simply for granted,[2] while others busied themselves in calculating the moons and speculating, for example, upon the identity of the three Kings who were to cast off the mantle of heresy.

---

[1] It would be useless to attempt any catalogue, but the following two books may be cited as typical specimens: Albert de Bec, *Henri V (le grand monarque) Restaurateur du Trône et des Gloires de la France et 80 ans de révolutions annoncés et jugés par les prophéties*, Paris, 1871; Abbé E. A. Chabauty, *Lettres sur les Prophéties modernes et Concordance de toutes les prédictions jusqu'au règne d'Henri V*, Poitiers, 1871. Both these works went through more than one edition. In another still more extravagant book, the Abbé H. Torné-Chavigny maintained that the real author of the Prophecy of Orval was Nostradamus; see *Lettres du Grand Prophète* (Paris), 1870, pp. 32 and 153.

[2] See, for example, Huguet, *Paris ses Crimes et ses Châtiments* (Lyons), pp. 81 and 94.

As all were agreed, the phrase " Woe to thee, great city," obviously referred to Paris, bombarded first of all by the enemy and then set on fire by the Commune. Not less unmistakably, so the same commentators insisted, was " the offspring of the Cap " (*i.e.*, the descendant of Hugh Capet) who " joined the lion to the white flower," to be identified with the person of the Comte de Chambord, Henri V. None the less, in 1871, when he had attained the age of 51, it was not easy to understand how he could be apostrophized as " Young Prince "; while, on the other hand, when the prophecy was given to the world before 1839 the phrase would have been natural enough, for the prospects of the boy known as the Comte de Chambord were already being discussed. The solitary feature in the document which could even for a moment be suspected of betraying any preternatural insight into the future is the curious prediction, " At this time two-thirds of a great people of the sea will return to the true faith." No Frenchman in 1832, it might be thought, could have dreamed of such a religious phenomenon as the Oxford movement. But promising as this utterance might have seemed amid the enthusiasm of the " Second Spring," not even the conversion of England, still less that of the three sovereigns, has yet been realized; while the Comte de Chambord has been in his grave for thirty years and the Pope is still a prisoner in the Vatican.

Nothing perhaps could more effectively illustrate the worthlessness of all this class of prophecies than the fact that already in the course of sixty years three successive interpretations have been adopted to determine the identity of this young Prince "the offspring of Hugh Capet." In the 'fifties a verification was sought in the dynasty of Napoleon III, and commentators were at pains to persuade their readers that the Prince Imperial and his mother the Empress Eugénie could claim through the family of Medina Coeli to be descended from Blanche, the daughter of St. Louis;[1] and now again when the hopes of the Chambord legitimists have suffered shipwreck there are still writers, incredible as it may appear, who cling to the Orval prediction, pointing out that "Louis XVII is still represented at the present moment (this was written in 1910) by six grandchildren, the sons of Prince Edmond and Adalbert de Bourbon."[2] According to M. Tisserant, then, the young prince, the offspring of the Cap, is still to come. None the less, to any impartial man who has the patience to look into the question of the prophecy of Orval, it must be perfectly plain that the document, though possibly incorporating older materials, was deliberately fabricated about the year 1832. The date is determined with all

[1] See Jeantin, *Les Ruines et les Chroniques de l'Abbaye d'Orval* (Paris, 1857), p. 224, note.
[2] H. Tisserant, *Voici l'Heure*, 8th ed. (Nancy, 1910), p. 44, note.

A Confession of Fraud

desirable accuracy by the language of paragraph 27: "Come, young prince, quit the island of captivity. Listen, unite the lion and the white flower." From 1830 to 1832 the youthful Henri V, who was 10 years old in 1830, was residing in Great Britain, and there was at that time every probability that he would continue to live there. It can hardly be doubted that by the "island of captivity" the prophet meant Great Britain, and that by the union of "the lion and the white flower" (*fleur-de-lys*) he intended to suggest the desirability of a matrimonial alliance between Henri V and the Princess Victoria, the future Queen of England.

The two facts, in any case, of which we have certain knowledge are these: First, that no printed text of the Prophecy of Orval has ever been produced which is older than 1839; and secondly, that in 1849 the Bishop of Verdun published a letter in which he condemned the Prophecy of Orval as a fraud, declaring that the fabricator was a priest of his own diocese who under pressure of a juridical examination had confessed his guilt.[1]

In spite of the grief caused by such a scandal, I have [wrote the Bishop] at least had the consolation of obtaining from the mouth of the culprit himself a complete admission of his fault. He declared to me, in fact, that the little book printed at Luxembourg

---

[1] This, we learn, was a certain Abbé Henri Dujardin who compiled a collection of prophecies in 1840, to which he gave the name of *L'Oracle*.

in 1544¹ had never existed, except in his own imagination, that the portion about the Empire [he means, of course, the first Empire, of Napoleon I] was entirely his work, that the rest had been pieced together at random from scraps of ancient prophecies, borrowed from various out-of-the-way collections, with regard to which I pronounce no opinion, that at the first he had no other intention in perpetrating this fraud than just to amuse himself, but that when some of his predictions chanced to come true, he had been led on, partly by vanity, partly by false shame, to persist in a deception from which he is now glad to be rescued.²

It is abundantly evident that such a letter could not have been written and published in the newspapers, if the confession of guilt spoken of therein had not been authentic. The Abbé H. Dujardin, the priest thus incriminated, was living at the time and made no protest. He was well known to have identified himself with the prophecy in print, and though the Bishop does not actually mention his name, he indicates him clearly by initials as " M. D. . . . Curé de B. . . ." But in spite of all this, as has been already noticed, the prophecy was not only

---

[1] In the preface to the early copies of the Prophecy of Orval this prediction was said to be contained in a little book published in 1544.

[2] At the time the Bishop's letter was penned the fullest publicity was given to it. It appeared in most of the Catholic newspapers, and notably in the *Journal de Bruxelles*, March 19th, 1849. Both this letter and the original preface to the Prophecy of Orval may be found in Migne, *Dictionnaire des Prophéties*, ii, 727. *Cf. Précis Historiques* (Brussels, 1870), vol. xix, p. 485.

Marie Lataste

revived in 1870, finding thousands of enthusiastic defenders, but it has also retained its credit with some strangely constituted intelligences down to our own day.

A word or two may be added about another prophecy which was much discussed in 1871-2, that of Marie Lataste, lay-sister of the Congregation of the Sacred Heart. The prediction is in any case noteworthy on this ground, that we possess beyond reasonable doubt the actual words of the mystic, not only dictated by herself at a date prior to the coming to pass of any of the events discussed, but published subsequently with ecclesiastical approbation. The exact year of the revelation cannot be assigned, but it must have happened upon some feast of the Immaculate Conception prior to 1843. Marie Lataste believed that on this occasion she was told by our Saviour that it was His will that the doctrine of the Immaculate Conception should be proclaimed on earth and acknowledged by all Christians. Our Lord then added: "I have chosen to Myself a Pope and I have inspired him with this resolution. He will ever have this thought in his mind from the time that he shall be Pope. He will collect together the Bishops of the whole world that their voices may be heard proclaiming Mary Immaculate in her Conception." Then Marie Lataste learnt from the same preternatural source that "affliction shall reign in the city which I love" [presumably

Rome]. "This city will seem to succumb during three years, and a little longer after these three years. But My Mother shall descend into the city; she will take the hands of the old man seated on a throne and will say to him, 'Behold the hour! arise, see thy enemies, I cause them to disappear one after another, and they disappear for ever. Thou shalt live, and I will live with thee. Old man, dry thy tears; I bless thee.'"[1]

Now it is unquestionable that Pius IX, who was elected in 1846, had the definition of the Immaculate Conception much at heart, and that he carried out his purpose in 1854. Of course, he may have known, and been influenced by, this prediction of Marie Lataste, but even so, the rapid fulfilment of the prophecy is sufficiently striking. Consequently when the papal government was overthrown in 1870 and Victor Emmanuel became master of Rome, those who remembered the holy lay-sister's words were confident that after the lapse of three years the Sovereign Pontiff would triumph over his enemies and that the temporal sovereignty would be restored to him. At about this period a new edition of Marie Lataste's writings and revelations was published with episcopal approbation, and the Vicar-General of the diocese of Aire (M. Guitton), together with another theologian,

[1] E. Healy Thompson, *Life of Marie Lataste* (1877), pp. 103-4, and *Letters and Writings* (Eng. ed., 1881), vol. i, p. 156.

committed themselves in print to the statement that for both of them "the decisive test of the truth of her prophecies will be the triumph of the present Pope and the deliverance of Rome."[1] Unfortunately the test failed; not only Pius IX, but two of his successors, have passed to their reward, and the triumph is apparently as far off as ever. Even the most robust champions of Marie Lataste's prophetic gifts must surely by this time have had their faith somewhat shaken.

Hardly less popular at the same epoch was the so-called Prophecy of Blois. If we could really trust the correctness of the text, which is supposed to have been communicated verbally to Mlle. de Leyrette, afterwards known as Mère Providence, by an Ursuline Tourière of Blois, called Sœur Marianne, in 1804, the prediction would be a very remarkable one; for many of its paragraphs seem to accord minutely with events which happened in 1820, 1830, and later on. But it is just here that the evidence is most unsatisfactory. Mère Providence was under the impression that she had been forbidden to write down any of the things that Sœur Marianne had told her. Consequently we have to trust to the memory of other members of the Blois Community who had heard some of the disconnected utterances which Mère Providence had passed on to them by word of mouth. In 1870, when this prophecy first began to attract attention,

[1] E. H. Thompson, *Life of Marie Lataste*, p. 340.

Mère Providence herself was 93 years old and incapable of giving any exact account of what she had heard sixty-six years before. But the general drift of the predictions pointed to a happy consummation in the near future, when France, after a period of desolating war and revolution, would enter upon a golden age of peace. For example:

Such wonderful things will happen that the most sceptical will be obliged to say that the finger of God is here.

You will sing a *Te Deum;* but talk of *Te Deums!*—I tell you that it will be such a *Te Deum* as has never been sung before.

It will take fifteen or twenty years for France to recover from her calamities.

However, things will settle down, and up to the time of perfect peace, until France shall have become more prosperous and tranquil than ever was known, some twenty years will roll by.

The triumph of religion will be such that no one has ever before seen its like. All wrongs will be set right, the laws of the State will be brought into harmony with those of God and the Church, the education given to children will be thoroughly Christian, and the guilds for workmen will be everywhere restored.[1]

Alas! not twenty, but forty, years have sped by since the epoch of the calamities—those of

---

[1] See especially F. Roux, *Examen de la Prophétie de Blois* (Paris, 1871), p. 33; and Richaudeau, *La Prophétie de Blois avec des Eclaircissements* (4th ed., Tours, 1872). *Cf. Précis Historiques* (1871), p. 91.

1870-1, which every commentator then declared to be the " grands événements " directly foretold by the prophetess—but the golden age of peace and the triumph of French Christianity has not yet arrived.

There can be no doubt that the Prophétie de Blois, which in its more approved form is a document of no great length, owed much of its vogue to a certain dramatic picturesqueness which characterizes it. Speaking apparently of the great conflict which was to precede the triumph of the Church, Sœur Marianne declared:

You will have to pray hard, for the wicked will seek to destroy everything. Before the great battle they will be masters; they will do all the harm they can, but not all they want to do, for they will not have time.

The great battle will be between the good and the wicked; it will be awful; the firing of the cannon will be heard for nine leagues round.

The good, being inferior in numbers, will be on the point of being exterminated; but—oh the power of God! oh the power of God!—the wicked will all perish. "Do you mean that all the wicked will perish, dear Marianne?" asked Mlle. de Leyrette. "Yes, and many of the good as well."

* * * * * *

When all is over three messengers will come. The first will brings news that all is lost. The second, who will arrive at night time, will find only a single man leaning against his doorway. "You are very hot, my friend," this man will say to him, "get down and have a glass of wine." "I am in too much of a hurry," the messenger will reply; and then he will ride on towards Le Berry.

You will all be at meditation when you will hear that two messengers have gone past; but then a third will arrive, *fire and water,*[1] who will tell you that the day is won; but he will have to be at Tours in an hour and a half.

There were many other prophecies in circulation in the days of the Franco-Prussian War, but we may be satisfied with having touched upon those which were most widely discussed. At the present time I note that the Prophecy of Orval still figures in a little brochure (undated, but from its contents obviously compiled or revised since the great war of 1914 began) which is now being sold in Paris.[2] Anna Maria Taigi and the Nun of Blois apparently offered nothing which the compiler found to his purpose, but from the Orval prediction he has extracted one sentence as bearing upon the present situation:

Come, young prince, leave the isle of captivity; unite the lion to the white flower.

This, the reader will be pleased to learn, is now interpreted as an invitation to his gracious Majesty King George V to unite under his

---

[1] The commentators are agreed that the good sister Marianne used this phrase in 1804 to convey that the news would come by train, a manner of locomotion she was unable to explain otherwise. The distance from Blois to Tours is about 35 miles.

[2] *Les Prédictions sur la Fin de l'Allemagne,* Editions et Librairie, Rue de Seine 40, Paris, fr.1.50.

leadership the armies of France and Belgium.[1] But why King George's island should be an "island of captivity" is a problem which is unfortunately left without explanation of any sort.

[1] *Prédictions sur la Fin de l'Allemagne*, p. 21.

CHAPTER II

THE PROPHETS AND ECCLESIASTICAL AUTHORITY

IT must not be supposed that the flood of prophetic literature of which we have just been speaking was allowed to circulate entirely without protest. Already in 1870, before the Franco-Prussian War had been more than a month or two in progress, a series of able articles, which rumour correctly attributed to Father Victor de Buck, S.J., the distinguished Bollandist, began to appear in the *Précis Historiques* of Brussels.[1] Not only did the writer himself deprecate strongly the credulity with which these prophecies were too commonly received, but he appealed to the praiseworthy example of prudence set by certain other religious periodicals which had not allowed themselves to be sucked into the vortex. Still more important was the pronouncement of the famous Bishop of Orléans, Mgr. Dupanloup, who since 1854 had been a member of the Académie française. A confer-

---

[1] " Des Prophéties en vogue "—the first article was printed in the *Précis* for October, 1870, pp. 479 *et seq.*, and it was followed by four others.

ence delivered by him on this subject was afterwards published as a pastoral under the title of *Lettre sur les prophéties contemporaines.* In this the Bishop tells his readers incidentally that he had had more than twenty books of this kind in his hands, and that he knew that of one of them, *Le Grand Avènement précédé du Grand Prodige,* more than 50,000 copies had been sold in a few weeks. But the main appeal of the letter is, of course, concerned with the regrettable effects produced upon the Christian life by the unrestrained indulgence of this appetite for the marvellous.

From all sides to-day [wrote the Bishop] we hear of nothing but miracles and prophecies, and to our generation also one may say what our Lord used once to say to His: "This generation seeketh a sign"—*Generatio ista signum quærit.* There is nothing to surprise us in this phenomenon. Periods of trouble, like ours, are its ordinary witnesses and causes. How much, indeed, in the midst of our sorrows have we not need of that token for good—*signum in bonum* (Ps. lxxxv. 17)—of which the Psalmist speaks? When great political and social commotions have upset men's minds, when unwonted calamities have fallen upon a people, when profound revolutions have shaken a nation to its very foundations, disturbed imaginations begin to work; they try to pierce the darkness of events, to catch a glimpse of the mysterious unknown hidden in the future, to discover at last the salvation long desired, the expected Saviour. Then the real, where nothing reassuring is seen, is surrendered for the imaginary, where everything is seen, especially what is hoped for. Prophets arise and wonder-workers too; visions, oracles, prodigies are multiplied; with fanatics in good faith knaves get mingled. Nevertheless, souls in their craving for light turn eagerly to any source which offers it, a curious ear is lent to those marvellous tales and to those voices[1] which profess to have come from on high; the credulous, and sometimes the sceptical themselves, through that deep need of penetrating the unknown which is inborn in the human soul, are swept off their feet; a whole generation feeds on chimeras, and at one time seized with vain fears trembles before the calamities announced as at the approach of the year 1000, at another following the dominant craze is filled with exultation, or goes to sleep without misgiving, buoyed up by hopes that are equally baseless.[2]

And since we are upon this topic, it may be well to supplement Mgr. Dupanloup's shrewd criticism by citing the text of certain conciliar decrees to which he rightly makes appeal as expressing the mind of the Church in the most authoritative manner. The first of these pronouncements was drawn up in the form of a papal bull during the fifth council of Lateran in 1516, *sacro approbante concilio*, and includes the following passage:[3]

[1] An obvious reference to the book previously spoken of, *Voix Prophétiques*. There were also German collections bearing the same title *Prophetenstimmen*.
[2] Dupanloup, *Lettre sur les Prophéties*, Eng. trans., p. 4. I have slightly modified the rendering there given.
[3] Harduin, *Concilia*, vol. ix, cols. 1808-9.

As regards the time at which the calamities to come are to happen, the coming of Antichrist and the day of judgment, let no one allow himself to announce them and to fix their date, for Truth has said that it is not for us to know the times or moments which the Father keeps in His own power. All who up to the present have dared to make such predictions have been found to be liars (*ipsos mentitos fuisse constat*), and it is certain that their conduct has done no small injury to the authority of those who are content to preach without predicting. For the future, then, we forbid all and any to announce future events in their public discourses by means of fanciful explanations of Holy Scripture, to pose as having received such instructions from the Holy Ghost or by a revelation from Heaven, and to set forth strange and vain divinations or things of that sort. . . . If, however, the Lord reveal to anyone by inspiration certain things to come to pass in the Church of God . . . as the matter is of great moment, seeing that no spirit is to be lightly believed, but spirits are to be proved, as the Apostle testifies, whether they are of God, we will that, in ordinary law, such alleged inspirations (*tales assertae inspirationes*), be understood to be henceforth reserved to the examination of the Apostolic See before being made public or preached to the people (*antequam publicentur aut populo prædicentur*). And if any dare in any way to contravene the premisses, besides the penalties provided by law against such, we will them to incur a sentence of excommunication also, from which they can be absolved only by the Roman Pontiff, except when at the point of death.

Although these warnings were immediately addressed to the popular preachers, who at a time of political excitement and religious decay scandalized many by their extravagances,[1] they nevertheless illustrate the attitude of ecclesiastical authority towards all such pretended revelations in general. Moreover, a comparatively modern decree, passed at Paris in a national council of all the French Bishops in 1849, and subsequently ratified by the Holy See, is still more to our purpose. Its enactment was obviously occasioned by the vogue of the prophecy of Orval and a number of similar predictions then current in France:

Since [said the Council] according to the Apostle not every spirit is to be believed, we warn our flocks that no one rashly set himself to spread the knowledge of prophecies, visions and miracles relating to politics, the future state of the Church or similar subjects, if published without their having been examined and approved by the Ordinary. Parish priests and confessors, in their prudence, will deter the faithful of Christ from a too easy acceptance of

---

[1] The example set by Savonarola some years before had been followed by a number of other popular preachers. Jerome of Bergamo in 1508 had announced to vast crowds that Italy would be devastated, and that Rome, Venice, and Milan would be destroyed by a nation hitherto unknown. A little later a Franciscan, Francesco da Montepulciano, produced a still more tremendous sensation by his prophecies of woes to come. He predicted that Rome would be laid waste, the clergy of evil life exterminated, that for three years there would be neither mass nor sermons, that the land would be bathed in blood, etc. See the account given by Pastor, *History of the Popes*, Eng. trans., vol. v, pp. 217 *et seq.*

them. They will also, as occasion offers, explain the rules prescribed by the Church on this subject, and especially will they admonish the faithful that their conduct is to be governed, not by private revelations, but by the ordinary laws of Christian wisdom.[1]

Neither must it be supposed that because the decrees most commonly appealed to are comparatively remote in date this legislation has fallen into desuetude. There is, for example, a section contained in the Constitution *Officiorum et munerum* of Pope Leo XIII (January 25th, 1897), which runs as follows:

Books and writings which recount new apparitions, revelations, visions, prophecies and miracles, or which introduce new devotions, even under the plea of their being for private use, supposing such to be published without the lawful permission of ecclesiastical authority, are forbidden.

Still more recent is an ordinance published by Mgr. Douais, Bishop of Beauvais, and embodied in a pastoral dated May 25th, 1912. It is interesting to note the provisions of this document, though, of course, its binding force is limited to the diocese for which it was issued:

i. We wish the most scrupulous reserve to be practised in the *forum externum* in regard to all stories of revelations, prophecies and miracles.

ii. If public notice be directed to such revelations, prophecies and miracles, we order them to be at once submitted to ecclesiastical authority.

[1] *Acta et Decreta, Collectio Lacensis*, vol. iv, p. 17.

iii. We forbid them to be communicated publicly to others, or to be propagated before they have been canonically pronounced upon or without our authorization.

iv. We forbid preachers either of the regular or secular clergy to introduce such stories into their sermons without first submitting them to ecclesiastical authority. The priests in charge of parishes are bound to make this prohibition known to preachers who are strangers.

v. Such stories must not be published either as books, or as articles in periodicals, without our permission, and we forbid the reading of them.

vi. When authorization is given to publish such stories the injunction of Urban VIII should be carefully observed.

vii. We ask pious persons, and our dear daughters the nuns of all religious communities, to be particularly on their guard in this matter. Whatever may be said to them, and whatever the degree of trust they repose in those who converse with them, they ought to be extremely reserved and prudent. The truest piety is that which is exact in observing the laws of the Church.

viii. We forbid the publication of all devotions and prayers unless they have been duly approved.[1]

No doubt all the Bishops did not in this matter hold the views here expressed by Mgr. Douais, and in the years which followed the Franco-Prussian War there was some difference of opinion and action among them regarding the

---

[1] See the *Revue du Clergé Français,* Aug. 1st, 1912, vol. lxii, p. 367.

An Archiepiscopal Imprimatur

ecclesiastical approval of books of prophecies. Father de Buck in 1870 was thoroughly justified in saying that for the most part these collections appeared without the sanction of authority. Even in the case of the *Voix Prophétiques,* which was less open to objection than some other publications of the same class, the three first editions bore no episcopal *imprimatur* of any kind. The fourth, however, had two or three letters prefixed which might be held to amount equivalently to an ecclesiastical approval. The fifth, published towards the close of 1872, bears a formal though somewhat guarded commendation signed by Mgr. Déchamps, Archbishop of Malines, in whose diocese the book was printed. His letter seems to throw the responsibility of approving such collections upon sundry articles which had appeared in the well-known Jesuit periodical of Italy, the *Civiltà Cattolica*.[1] These articles directed attention to the predictions as documents which deserved to be treated seriously and which might usefully help to inspire confidence in the hearts of despondent believers. Probably the Archbishop felt that it would be tactful to entrench himself against such criticisms as those of Father de Buck by invoking the example of the Jesuit Father's own religious brethren who, living under the shadow of the Vatican, were believed to be almost more papal

[1] See in particular *Civiltà Cattolica,* March 22nd, 1872, pp. 526 *et seq.,* and April 23rd, 1872, pp. 291 *et seq. Cf.* November 17th, 1871, p. 529, and July 2nd, 1854, pp. 1 *et seq.*

than the Pope himself. It must be confessed that these *Civiltà* articles are now rather pitiable reading. The trust reposed in such predictions as those of Marie Lataste, Anna Maria Taigi, and in the still more apocryphal utterances attributed to St. Cæsarius of Arles, Jerome Bottin, and David Paré,[1] teach a painful lesson as to the fallibility of the guidance afforded by the learned editors. It becomes plain that in matters in which the wish was the father to the thought, neither all their orthodoxy nor all their theological learning could save them from egregious self-deception.

Speaking generally, however, very few of the books of prophecies, especially at first, appeared with any sort of *imprimatur,* and the enthusiasts who, with more or less of good faith, were keenly interested in propagating these revelations of the future, realized the advantage of associating them as far as possible with names which all the religious world held in veneration. Sometimes this result was attained by attributing the prophecies themselves to saintly authors like St. Bridget, St. Cæsarius, the Curé d'Ars, the Abbé Eymard, etc., sometimes by inducing priests who were exceptionally respected to take an active part in the propagation of this kind of literature. A remarkable example of the latter procedure may be noticed in the case of the

[1] All these writers were quoted in justification of the belief that the triumph of the Church might be expected in the near future during the pontificate of Pius IX himself.

The Saint of Toulouse

well-known Capuchin missioner, Father Marie-Antoine (Clergue), whose Life, a volume of 680 pages royal 8vo, has recently been published under the title of *Le Saint de Toulouse*.[1] The good Father's biographer, while skating as rapidly as possible over thin ice, does not disguise the fact that the holy Capuchin was the compiler of one of the most famous of these collections of prophecies, that known as *Le grand Pape et le grand Roi*. He evidently feels that some sort of explanation is called for, and thus in speaking of the nightmare of discouragement and irreligion which had settled down on France after the war of 1870, the biographer just referred to tells us that all good Frenchmen eagerly looked forward to happier times, adding that

While the wiser of them were content to wait for events to develop, the more ardent spirits, eager to anticipate the coming of the dawn, turned their thoughts heavenwards and consulted the future. In response to this state of popular feeling, which was widespread in France at the time, an immense number of predictions were dragged to light out of old books, or legends of more or less doubtful authenticity. The great body of Catholics believed in them. The most sober newspapers, the *Univers* and the various *Semaines Catholiques*, joined in giving them currency, priests of high standing guaranteed them authentic. These prophecies gratified a craving almost universally felt. The

[1] *Le Saint de Toulouse, Vie du Père Marie-Antoine*, O.F.M.C., par P. Ernest-Marie de Beaulieu (Toulouse, 1908).

present outlook was so gloomy that men were driven to find consolation in hopes, which, alas! were no more than phantoms, and which only led to further disappointment.[1]

One of the most ardent collectors of these prophetic utterances was, it appears, a certain Father Fulgentius, an enthusiastic royalist and supporter of the Bourbon claims, who was then also a member of the Capuchin community at Toulouse. From him were derived the materials for the two volumes which the saintly Père Marie-Antoine published under the titles of *Le grand Pape et le grand Roi* and *Le prochain Dénouement de la Crise actuelle*. The biographer just quoted tells us that of all the brochures of which Père Marie-Antoine was the author these two had the greatest sale. Even a member of the French episcopate, Mgr. Epivent, Bishop of Aire, wrote enthusiastically to the author when the second of these two works appeared:

> I have drained it at a draught as one drinks from a goblet full of a beverage unknown, but most refreshing. It has left a flavour of piety behind, and also a steadfast spirit to encounter the terrors with which we are threatened.

Unhappily, the Great Monarch, Henri V, whose glorious reign these prophecies professed to announce, died in 1883, and by this fact it was made clear that "the saint of Toulouse," in spite of his personal holiness, was by no means

---

[1] *Le Saint de Toulouse*, p. 367.

divinely inspired when he encouraged his countrymen to attach credence to these fallacious predictions.

Naturally the holiness of the author of a prophecy was held to be a point of even more importance than the holiness of those who put faith in it. We cannot, therefore, be surprised to find that the authority of such a man as the Curé d'Ars was widely invoked to lend credit to the dream of a renovated France, a triumphant Christian monarchy, and a pope reinstated in his temporal jurisdiction. This particular attempt to invest the alluring but baseless vision with a religious sanction has the better claim to our attention because the same materials were served up again in the September of 1914, and were supposed to find their true fulfilment in the events of the military drama then being enacted. The whole process is worth studying as an illustration of the mentality of those who put faith in revelations of this kind.

Although the accredited biographers of the Blessed Jean Marie Vianney attribute to him a remarkable prophetic gift, often exercised for the benefit of individual souls who consulted him, they are silent as to any disclosures of future political events. It was a fixed principle with the holy Curé to concern himself as little as possible with such matters of public interest. The sanctification of his own soul and the help of his neighbours absorbed all his time. The fact then remains that all these alleged predictions of the Curé d'Ars which were so keenly discussed in 1871 and in 1914 depend simply upon the testimony of a young lay-brother unnamed, who, as the political crisis of the Franco-Prussian War grew more and more grave, professed to recall in more and more detail what had been told him by the Curé in the course of two interviews some twelve or fifteen years earlier. If we had to depend entirely upon the information of the Abbé Curicque, the compiler of the *Voix Prophétiques*, we should not even know to what religious congregation this lay-brother belonged; but in the *Grand Pape et grand Roi* of Père Marie-Antoine we learn that he was a member of the Lazarist Order. That the recollections of this anonymous brother, unsupported by any other evidence, oral or documentary, should have been so readily credited and should have supplied material for discussion to thousands of Catholics and even unbelievers, is alone a curious revelation of the keenness of the popular appetite for the marvellous. But the manner in which the so-called prophecy was revived and re-cast forty-three years later to fit quite another set of circumstances is even more instructive. Perhaps the simplest way of making the matter intelligible will be to translate the relevant data from the pages of the Abbé Curicque in the order in which they were taken down by the members of the lay-brother's own community.

It appears, then, that on September 7th, 1870 (Sedan, it will be remembered, was fought on September 2nd of that year) the lay-brother told his confrères something of the predictions which he had heard, as he maintained, from the lips of the venerated Curé himself shortly before his death in August, 1859. We may note as an instructive fact, that at first the community admittedly paid no heed to these communications.[1] This seems to show that they did not usually regard the narrator as a very serious or trustworthy person. We are expressly informed that it was only towards the end of the siege of Paris that they could be persuaded to listen to him with any attention. However, when the siege was already over, that is in February, 1871, a formal statement of these disclosures was drawn up, which the lay-brother afterwards signed. Most of this statement relates to the brother's vocation to the Lazarists and to the history of the house in which he lived, but some other rather obscure utterances seem to refer to the siege of Paris by the Prussians, as well as to the capitulation of the city, the surrender of weapons, and to the difficulty in obtaining provisions. Then the account goes on:

The Brother also added that M. Vianney told him: "It will not last long. People will think that all is lost, but the Bon Dieu will make everything

[1] *Voix Prophétiques,* 5th ed., vol. ii, p. 177. No mention of this incredulity occurs in the 3rd ed.

right. It will be a sign of the last Judgment. Paris will be transformed, and also two or three other cities. They will want to canonize me, but they will not have time for it.'"[1]

From Abbé Curicque's account it plainly appears that this passage was already an addition to the brother's original statement. But at the beginning of March, 1871, he had still further recollections to communicate. The Abbé Curicque, when making these public in the autumn of 1871, remarks that this further supplement, like that just quoted, must plainly have reference to events which at that date had not yet come to pass.

The enemy will not quit the country altogether.[2] They will come back again, and they will destroy everything on their line of march. No resistance will be offered; they will be allowed to advance, but after that their supplies will be cut off and they will suffer great losses. They will retire towards their own country, but we shall follow them up, and not many of them will ever reach home.

---

[1] *Voix Prophétiques*, 5th ed., vol. ii, p. 182. In the version printed by Père Marie-Antoine other details are added in this same context. Lyons and Marseilles are named as other cities that would be transformed, and it is stated that " God shall come to help, the good shall triumph when the return of the King (Henri V) shall be announced. This shall re-establish a peace and prosperity without example. Religion shall flourish again better than ever before." See *The Christian Trumpet* (London, 1875), p. 88.

[2] It is important to remember that when this was first committed to writing in 1871, the war was indeed over, but many Prussian garrisons were still left in France to secure the observance of the conditions of peace.

Then we shall recapture everything that they have carried off, and plenty more besides.¹

According to Père Marie-Antoine's version the lay brother here spoke not of the "enemy" but of the "Prussians." He also declared that the Prussians would advance as far as Poitiers, 300 miles south-west of Paris, and that the "papal zouaves of Cathelineau and Charette would cover themselves with glory."

But not even yet were the brother's recollections entirely exhausted. In November, 1871, too late for this third edition of the *Voix Prophétiques*, Abbé Curicque received from the Lazarists these further details, written down some time in August, concerning M. Vianney's communication to the lay brother fifteen years before.

The crisis is not over yet (*la grosse affaire n'est pas passée*). Paris will be demolished and burnt in earnest, but not entirely. Events will happen more terrible than anything we have yet seen (he refers presumably to the siege and the period of the Commune). However, there will be a limit beyond which the destruction will not go.

Asked what kind of limit was meant, the brother declared he did not know: "But," he added, "we shall come through all right (*pourtant nous serons en deçà*), and I should not think of leaving the house." By this time the brother, who according to his own fellow reli-

---
¹ *Voix Prophétiques*, 3rd ed., p. 349.

gious, was a simple countryman who in general knew little of the news of the day, had heard of the indemnity and of the Prussian garrisons that were to remain in France until the indemnity was paid. At any rate, it was only at this date (August, 1871)[1] that he represented the Curé d'Ars as having finally said to him:

"They will want them to leave sooner, but the enemy will demand more money or some other concession, and they will come back. This time it will be a fight to a finish (*on se battra pour tout de bon*); for on the first occasion our soldiers did not fight well, but then they will fight; oh! how they will fight! The enemy, it is true, will let Paris burn, and they will be well pleased with themselves, but we shall smash them and put them to flight for good and all (*et on les chassera pour tout de bon*). I don't know (added the holy Curé) why I tell you all this, but when the time comes you will remember it, and you will be quite easy in your mind, as well as those who shall believe you."[2]

To anyone who pays attention to the sequence and the wording of these communications, it became abundantly plain that the brother believed (what so many other Frenchmen believed, while Prussian garrisons still remained on French soil and the payments of the war indemnity were still being made), that the five milliards of French gold once delivered over would only

[1] *Voix Prophétiques,* 4th ed., vol. ii, p. 172; 5th ed., vol. ii, p. 183.
[2] *Ibid.*

whet the Prussian appetite for more. The opportunity would soon come (*ce ne sera pas long*), a pretext would be found for fresh demands, the Prussians would again invade France, Paris would be burned, but God in the end would intervene and the enemy would have to disgorge all they had taken.

Now, in September, 1914, those who endeavoured to apply this prediction to the campaign then begun cannot fail to have seen the weak points of such an interpretation. But they took certain sentences apart from their context,[1] and some of the more unscrupulous deliberately added a clause to the original, naming a feast of Our Lady (the Nativity of the Blessed Virgin, September 8th) as the turning point of the campaign. Of this clause concerning the feast of Our Lady there is not a trace either in the version of the Abbé Curicque or even in what he describes as the interpolated text of Père Marie-Antoine. Still, in the following adaptation, which was widely circulated in September, 1914, the prophecy sounded highly impressive:

The enemy will not retire immediately. They will again return, destroying as they come. Effective resistance will not be offered them. They will be allowed to advance, but after that their communications will be cut off, and they will suffer great losses. They will then retire towards their own country, but they will be followed, and not many will reach their

[1] See for example the brochure *Les Prédictions sur la Fin de L'Allemagne* (Paris, 1914), p. 20.

goal. They will then restore what they have taken away, and more in addition. Much more terrible things will happen than have yet been seen. Paris will suffer, but a great triumph will be witnessed on the Feast of Our Lady.[1]

To those who still continue to treat this prediction seriously one can only point out that, according to the express terms of the lay brother's account, Paris was to be burned down before the hour of triumph came. Paris has not been burned down, and it is consequently quite impossible to identify the change of fortune which began about the 8th of September, 1914, with the final victory foreshadowed by the Lazarist lay-brother. It is difficult to resist the conviction that the brother, no doubt in all good faith, had come to read his own dreams into a somewhat vague recollection of his conversations with the holy Curé. At any rate, as the prophecy stood in 1872, and as it was unanimously interpreted by its editors at that date, it is certain that the prediction was not fulfilled.

Not unlike the forecast attributed to the Blessed Jean Marie Vianney is that fathered upon the saintly Dom Bosco, the founder of the Salesians. The motive, viz., to secure the appearance of high religious sanction for an encouraging prognostic, was no doubt the same in each case; but while the prophecy assigned to

[1] See, *e.g.*, the *Daily Chronicle* and several other English newspapers.

The Dom Bosco Fabrication

the Curé d'Ars has at least some shadow of foundation in the recollections of the Lazarist lay-brother, the prediction circulated under the name of Dom Bosco seems to have been a deliberate imposture. In fact, the whole setting of the document proclaims its suspicious character. It appeared in many English and foreign newspapers, but I quote it here exactly as it stands in the *Occult Review* for October, 1914:

As I go to press yet another prediction of the present war reaches me, this time from Norway, though the author of the prediction is stated to have been a Portuguese priest by the name of Dom Bosco, who died ten years ago, and the quotation is a translation from the well-known French paper, *Le Matin*, in which it appeared in June, 1901. It runs as follows:

"In 1913 or 1914 a great European War will break out. Germany will be torn completely to pieces, but not before the Germans have penetrated into the heart of France, whence they will be forced back to the further banks of the Rhine. An arrogant man will see his family tree cut in splinters and trampled upon by all the world. Great battles will take place on August 15th and September 15th. At that time the Pope will die and live again, and become stronger than ever. Poland will get back her rights."

Now to begin with, Dom Bosco was not a Portuguese priest, neither did he die ten years ago. A Piedmontese[1] by birth, he died in Turin

---

[1] It is possible that in some manuscript copy "Piedmontese" was written, but misread "Portuguese." On the other hand, Father Macey tells me that he has heard of another Dom Bosco who was of Portuguese nationality.

in January, 1888. The only point which would lead one to think the prophecy worthy of a moment's consideration is the explicit statement that this prediction containing an announcement of the Pope's death in August or September at the beginning of a great European war was published in *Le Matin* in 1901. A friend of mine who had the curiosity to write to the Paris office of *Le Matin* to make inquiries, sent on to me the letter he received in answer. The letter simply stated that *Le Matin* had published no such prophecy. This may be taken as conclusive, and it seems useless to attempt to pursue the matter further. The more so that, in answer to my inquiries, the Very Rev. C. B. Macey, the Rector of the Salesian School at Battersea, has kindly informed me that according to the unanimous testimony of their older Fathers there was no ground for attributing such a prediction to their venerable founder.

CHAPTER III

"BROTHER JOHANNES"

THE predictions discussed in the last chapter have already brought us into contact with the European war of 1914, and we may now appropriately occupy ourselves with the most audacious of the many attempts to exploit popular credulity which have been occasioned by that great political crisis. The "Prophecy of Brother Johannes," originally published in the *Figaro*,[1] has attracted an enormous amount of attention, and has been translated into almost all European languages. It has reached even the English local newspapers, and has been sold separately in many forms. But despite all this publicity and the strenuous efforts of devout believers, it remains as completely destitute of external confirmation as when it was first made known. There are sundry people who declare vaguely that they have seen it in print years ago; but no definite book has been produced which contains it, nor has even the title been

---

[1] September 10th, 1914, and September 17th, 1914. *Cf.* also the issue for September 26th.

"Brother Johannes"

quoted of any such work. So far as the public at large are concerned, the prophecy of "Brother Johannes" may be said to have dropped from the clouds. No single detail in the account given of it has been verified or seems capable of verification. But let us turn at once to the document itself, which, according to M. Joséphin Péladan, who found it and edited it for the *Figaro*, is translated from a Latin original written somewhere about the year 1600.

THE ANTICHRIST

1. People will many times have imagined that they recognized him, for all the slayers of the Lamb are alike and all evil-doers are the precursors of the supreme evil-doer.

2. The true Antichrist will be one of the monarchs of his time, a son of Luther. He will call upon the name of God and will give himself out to be His messenger.

3. This prince of liars will swear by the Bible. He will pose as the arm of the Almighty, chastising a corrupt age.

4. He will be a one-armed man, but his soldiers without number, whose motto will be "God with us," will resemble the legions of hell.

5. For a long space he will work by cunning and crime, and his spies will infest the whole earth, and he will make himself master of the secrets of the mighty.

6. He will have theologians in his pay who will certify and demonstrate that his mission is from on high.

The Antichrist of To-day 49

7. A war will furnish him with the opportunity for throwing off the mask. It will not be the war that he will wage against a French sovereign, but another which will be easily recognized by this mark, that within a fortnight all the world will be involved in it.

8. It will set all Christian peoples by the ears, as well as all the Mohammedans and other nations far remote. In all the four quarters of the world armies will muster.

9. For the angels will open men's minds, and in the third week they will come to see that it is Antichrist, and that they will all be made slaves if they do not overthrow this hell-begotten tyrant.

10. Antichrist will be known by many signs. He will above all put to the sword priests, monks, women, children, and old men. He will show no pity. He will sweep onward, a blazing torch in his hand, like the barbarians of old, but the name of Christ will be on his lips.

11. His deceitful words will be like those of the Christians, but his acts will resemble those of Nero and the Roman persecutors. There will be an eagle in his coat of arms, as there is also in that of his lieutenant, the other wicked emperor.

12. But this latter is a Christian, and he will die of the curse of Pope Benedict who will be elected at the beginning of the reign of Antichrist.

13. Priests and monks will no longer be seen to hear confessions and to absolve the combatants; partly because for the first time priests and monks will fight like their fellow-citizens, partly because Pope Benedict having cursed Antichrist, it will be proclaimed that those who fight against him are in a

state of grace, and if they die go straight to heaven as the martyrs do.

14. The Bull that proclaims these things will produce a great sensation; it will re-enkindle the courage of the faint-hearted, and it will cause the death of the monarch allied with Antichrist.

15. Before Antichrist is overthrown more men will have to be killed than were ever contained within the walls of Rome. All kingdoms will have to unite in the task, for the cock, the leopard, and the white eagle would never get the better of the black eagle if the prayers and vows of all mankind did not come to their support.

16. Never will mankind have had to face such a danger, because the triumph of Antichrist would be that of the spirit of evil who has taken flesh in him.

17. For it has been said that twenty centuries after the Incarnation of the Word, the Beast in his turn will become incarnate, and will threaten the earth with as many horrors as the Divine Incarnation has brought blessings.

Here the first instalment of the prophecy stopped, and a paragraph was added to explain with quite unnecessary insistence, that the prediction could not have been meant to apply to the war 1870-1, but that its many indications were only verified in the later war. After which the reader was told:

There are people who reject all prophecies. But who can fail to be moved by the agreement in so many precise details and at three hundred years' interval between the predictions of Brother Johannes and the events going on around us?

The prophecy of Brother Johannes does not end here, it contains a terrible second part; but this last promises an era of peace and of light for France and all the world, and before this era is reached a vengeance so frightful that it even goes beyond men's thoughts or desires.

This article attracted an amount of attention which must have been highly gratifying both to the contributor himself and to the editor of the *Figaro*. Accordingly a week later another instalment was launched, consisting, like its predecessor, of exactly seventeen paragraphs and with a curious completeness and unity of its own, as if the prophet three centuries before had foreseen that his vaticinations were going to be published in the form of short newspaper articles. We may call this second part, though this is not the title given it by M. Péladan, by the name of—

THE BATTLE OF THE BEASTS

18. Somewhere about the year 2000 Antichrist will stand revealed; his armies will exceed in number anything that can be imagined. There will be Christians amongst his hordes, and there will be Mohammedan and pagan soldiers among the defenders of the Lamb.

19. For the first time the Lamb will be entirely red, in the whole of the Christian world there will not be a single spot that will not be red; and the heavens, the earth, the water, and even the air will be red, for blood will flow in the sphere of the four elements at the same time.

20. The black eagle will throw itself upon the cock, which will lose many of its feathers, but will strike heroically with its spur. It would soon be exhausted were it not for the help of the leopard and its claws.

21. The black eagle, which will come from the land of Luther, will surprise the cock from another side, and will invade one-half of the land of the cock.

22. The white eagle, which will come from the north, will set upon the black eagle and the other eagle, and will invade the land of the Antichrist from one end to the other.

23. The black eagle will find itself compelled to let the cock go in order to fight the white eagle, and the cock will pursue the black eagle into the land of Antichrist to help the white eagle.

24. The battles waged until then will be trifling in comparison to those that will take place in the land of Luther, because the seven angels will at the same time pour fire from their censers on the impious land (image taken from the Apocalypse), which means that the Lamb will order the extermination of the race of Antichrist.

25. When the Beast sees that he is lost he will become furious. It is ordained that for months together the beak of the white eagle, the claws of the leopard, and the spurs of the cock must tear his vitals.

26. Rivers will be forded over masses of dead bodies, which in some places will change the course of the waters. Only great noblemen, generals, and princes will receive burial, for to the carnage caused by firearms will be added the heaps and heaps of those who perish by famine and plague.

The Punishment of Antichrist

27. Antichrist will ask for peace again and again, but the seven angels who precede the three animals, defenders of the Lamb, have declared that victory shall only be accorded upon condition that Antichrist be crushed, like straw on a threshing-floor.

28. Executors of the justice of the Lamb, the three animals cannot stop fighting as long as Antichrist has a soldier left to defend him.

29. The reason why the sentence of the Lamb is so ruthless is that Antichrist has claimed to be a Christian and to be acting in His Name, so that if he did not perish the fruit of the redemption would be lost, and the gates of Hell would prevail against the Saviour.

30. It will be seen that this combat, which will be fought out where Antichrist forges his arms, is no human contest. The three animals, defenders of the Lamb, will exterminate Antichrist's last army; but the battlefield will become as a funeral pyre, larger than the greatest of cities, and the corpses will have changed the very features of the landscape through the ridges of mounds with which it will be covered.

31. Antichrist will lose his crown, and will die abandoned and insane. His Empire will be divided up into twenty-two States, but none will have either a stronghold, an army or ships of war.

32. The white eagle, by Michael's order, will drive the Crescent from Europe, where none but Christians will remain; he will instal himself in Constantinople.

33. Then an era of peace and prosperity will begin for all the universe, and there will be no more war,

each nation being governed according to its wish and living in justice.

34. There will be no more Lutherans or Schismatics. The Lamb will reign, and the bliss of human race will begin. Happy they who escaping from the perils of this prodigious time can taste of its fruit, which will be the reign of the Holy Spirit and the sanctification of humanity, only to be accomplished after the defeat of Antichrist.

It can be hardly necessary to point out that by the Cock France is indicated, by the Leopard England, by the White Eagle Russia, and by the Black Eagle and the other Eagle Germany and Austria.

On reading this document it seems almost incredible that it can ever have been considered in any other light than that of a hoax or a *mauvaise plaisanterie*. But many persons regard it seriously, and among them not only simple-hearted nuns and pious women who would consider a forgery in these matters as little better than a sacrilege, but also enthusiasts of a much more robust mentality. Its fictitious character, to my thinking, cannot for a moment be in doubt, though it is possible that in the first instance it may have been fabricated to deride rather than to mislead.

To begin with, it lacks any sort of reliable authentication. We have nothing more than M. Péladan's assurance that he found it among his father's papers after the death of the latter,

The Provenance of the Document

which took place in 1890. It is further stated that the prophecy was given to M. Adrien Péladan, *père*, by a Premonstratensian monk of S. Michel de Trigolet, near Tarascon (ominous name), who in his turn had received it from an Abbé Donat, a learned priest, who died at an advanced age at Beaucaire. For all this, however, we have no evidence except the declaration of M. Josephin Péladan, who in all probability makes no scruple of availing himself of a novelist's privilege to invent a pedigree for his fictions. Romance writers from Sir Walter Scott downwards have always been fertile in such expedients. As for the supposed author, Brother Johannes, no information is furnished regarding his manner of life or the place in which he lived, or the Order to which he belonged, or the circumstances under which this revelation was made to him. In glancing through some thirty odd volumes of this kind of literature which I have been able to consult, I have not come upon the least trace of Brother Johannes' wonderful seventeenth century prophecy. Neither can I recall more than one or two that even affect the same precision of detail. Let us note how marvellously minute the information is. Antichrist is to be an Emperor who makes a parade of his devotion to the Bible, who has theologians in his pay to draw up manifestos, and who is leagued with another Emperor near to death. Further, he has only the use of one arm, he is a hypocrite, and he has vast armies under his control, whose motto is "God with us." During his time a Pope shall be elected called Benedict. In the universal war that breaks out and embraces both East and West, no mercy shall be shown to priests and nuns, and numbers of priests, for the first time in history, shall take part as combatants (v. 13). Even Mohammedans and pagans shall be found in the ranks of those opposing Antichrist (v. 18). The war also will be fought in the air as well as on land and sea (v. 19). Can it be conceived that to this absolutely unknown monk of the seventeenth century the Almighty should have given such marvellous prophetic insight as is not to be paralleled in all the recorded history of the canonized saints? I would confidently challenge the production of one well attested example, either of saint, mystic, or seer which in any way rivals the foreknowledge displayed by Brother Johannes. We know what the scriptural prophecies are like, and we may easily acquaint ourselves with the language of the authentic prophetical writings of saints like St. Hildegard, St. Bridget, or St. Catherine of Siena. In this matter one of the very collections against which we are protesting lays down quite soberly the following canon as a means of distinguishing genuine prophecies from the spurious:

Genuine prophecies have a prophetic form. They are set forth in marvellous images in dark mysterious

The Personality of Sar Péladan 57

words; they often bring together totally dissimilar events, invert occasionally the order of time; while their authors, overpowered with the general impression of their visions employ exaggerated language. For instance "the blood will mount even to the horses' bridles." From these peculiarities we see that a certain obscurity attaches to prophecies. But this very quality bespeaks their divine origin, as hereby they seem to bear a certain conformity to the other works of God. In nature and history also God conceals Himself in order that those only who seek Him in faith may find Him.[1]

Moreover, the gravest suspicion is thrown upon the document under discussion, owing to the fact that at its first appearance in print, which occurred, as already stated, in the *Figaro* of September 10th and 17th, 1914, it was introduced to the world by that extraordinary genius, M. Josephin Péladan, whose talent is undeniable, but who may be described as a medley of Richard Wagner, Cagliostro, and Madame Blavatsky rolled into one. Here is the account of him in Curinier's *Dictionnaire national des Contemporains*.[2]

PELADAN, JOSEPHIN called "le Sar" (*i.e.*, the Seer), novelist, art-critic and dramatic author, born at Lyons 20 October, 1859. The son of a religious writer,[3] he has devoted himself to a style of litera-

---

[1] Beykirch, *Prophetenstimmen mit Erklärungen*, Paderborn, 1849, p. 7.
[2] Vol. v, p. 15, 1905.
[3] M. Adrien Péladan, *père*, was for many years editor of the *Semaine religieuse* of Lyons. There was also an Adrien Péladan, *fils*, the brother of Josephin.

ture which is partly mystic and partly erotic, while the titles he has bestowed upon himself of Mage and Seer serve to direct attention to his own personality, just as his wish to seem different from the rest of the world is made clear to all by his eccentricities of manner and costume.[1]

In the same notice, after a long list of his novels, plays, and other works, we are told that " M. Péladan founded the Order of the Rosy Cross, Cross of the Temple, of which he appointed himself Grand-Master." No doubt the Seer identifies himself with the cause of Catholicity, or at any rate Christianity, but his creed seems to be one peculiar to himself in which Occultism plays a larger part than revelation.[2] On the other hand, it is quite true that M. Péladan's father was, as stated, a collector of prophecies, particularly in the Catholic and Legitimist interest, and that he published in 1871 a book entitled *Le nouveau " Liber mirabilis," ou toutes les prophéties authentiques sur les temps présents*, with some other collections of the same kind.

---

[1] M. Péladan, it appears, loves to attire himself in long robes or oriental fashion and texture, while his portraits are evidently designed to produce the effect of a Blavatsky-like intensity of expression. All the resources of photography have been invoked to emphasize the dilated pupils, which seem to read into the soul and penetrate the future.

[2] Here is a specimen of one of his utterances, which, for fear of misinterpretation, I copy untranslated: " L'occulte est l'esprit même de la religion et la religion est le corps même de l'occulte. L'occulte est la tête où se conçoit le mystère, la religion est le cœur où le mystere se dynamise." Péladan, *L'Occulte Catholique.*

An Accommodating Editor 59

Taken as a whole, the explanations which M. Péladan has offered concerning the prophecy of Brother Johannes have only served to throw more suspicion upon the document itself. When it first appeared in the *Figaro* he let it be understood that he himself had translated it from the Latin (*j'ai trouvé à la traduire et à l'éclaircir*). Later he declared that he had done no more than to eliminate a few verbal redundancies (*je n'ai fait que serrer un peu l'expression*).[1] Certain it is, in any case, that not a phrase now survives which suggests a Latin original. On the other hand, M. Péladan tells us that out of consideration for republican susceptibilities he omitted sundry references to " the great monarch, the offspring of the lilies " to whom in the text the final defeat of Antichrist is attributed, also that he " bitterly regretted not having struck out all mention of the present Pope, the *religio depopulata* of St. Malachy." But it is just by this free-and-easy attitude towards an historical document that the editor forfeits all our confidence. Either the name of Pope Benedict was in the copy left by M. Péladan, *père*, or it was not. If it was not, his son, by inserting it in the text without warning of any kind, has committed a literary fraud which is absolutely unpardonable. On the other hand, if the name of the present pontiff stood

[1] See the *Figaro*, September 26th, 1914, and the prophecy in leaflet form published at the " Librairie Moderne," 5, Rue du Pont-de-Lodi, Paris.

revealed in a document copied by M. Péladan, *père,* before his death in 1890, the fact is marvellous beyond example, and to suppress such a circumstance in editing the document would be to deprive the prophecy of its supreme authentication. As the whole of M. Péladan's commentary shows, his mind is fixed, not upon what is true, but upon what is expedient, *i.e.,* what will best help to enkindle the fury of his countrymen against the German invader. This attitude alone would let us clearly see what we have to expect from him.

Again, M. Péladan informs his readers that what he has published " is only a section (*une tranche*) of a long prophecy which extends with occasional breaks from the sixteenth to the twentieth century." Surely, if he were really serious, the Seer could not be so lacking in perception as to be blind to the prodigious interest of all this. Even were the document no older than 1890, such a forecast of fighting in the air, theologians' manifestos, combatant priests, a newly-elected Pope named Benedict, etc., would make it, as already pointed out, the most wonderful prophecy ever heard of. But supposing it to date from 1600, the revelation becomes stupendous. There would not be a word of this marvellous text which we could spare. We should want to have it all before us in facsimile in order that from the measure of its fulfilment in the past we might learn how far we might rely with safety upon its exhilarating promise of victory in the future.

But it is absurd to labour the point. M. Péladan, in spite of his fantastic *allures,* is much too shrewd a man to be blind to all this. It is probable enough that he found among his father's papers some rather lurid prediction concerning Antichrist and a great battle in which the cock and the leopard all played their parts. There were hundreds of such documents circulating in the seventeenth century—extracts from one or two will be given later on—and since then the number has continually been added to. From the evidence of a certain Madame Faust[1] it is clear enough that more than twenty years ago M. Péladan was accustomed to deliver some such " Prophecy of the Twentieth Century " as a recitation. A seer has to justify his seership. France dreamed of the *revanche* long before 1890, and an identification of the Lutheran monarch with Antichrist, a figurative description of an awful conflict among the beasts ending with the victory of France and the Lamb would have been readily welcomed by most of the audiences which M. Péladan had to address. No doubt he at that time acquired the habit—there was no particular reason why he should not—of adapting the details of his weird prophetic rhapsody to the hopes and sympathies of

---

[1] See the *Occult Review,* December, 1914, p. ii, and *Light,* December 5th and 12th, pp. 587 and 594.

his hearers. Naturally enough the crisis of last September revived the idea in his mind, and, lo! we have a hastily elaborated recension[1] of the old Antichrist prophecy, adjusted to modern conditions, appearing in the columns of the *Figaro*. There is not a scrap of evidence forthcoming to show that any one of the really significant features of the present document, *e.g.*, the name of the Pope, the priests as combatants, the contest in the air, etc., is older than the declaration of war in August, 1914. Be it noted also in passing, à propos of the contest in the air (v. 19) that the enumeration of the four elements involves a blunder of which no seventeenth century author could possibly have been guilty. I hold, then, that the significant part of the prediction is of the same alloy as the prophecy of Orval and other similar fabrications. The foundation document may be relatively ancient, but even this has very probably been modified in transmission in accordance with the ideas of those who copied it or edited it. For this reason I do not think that we can attach the slightest importance to the statements of those who vaguely assert that they

---

[1] The signs of carelessness in the adaptation are unmistakable. From v. 7 it is plain that the original prophet, if he identified Antichrist with any German Emperor, identified him with William I; only William I could have "made war on a French sovereign." Again v. 12 declares that the new Pope is to be elected at the *beginning* of the reign of Antichrist, but William II succeeded to the throne in 1888. Further, the date "about the year 2000" (v. 18) is utterly irreconcilable with either William I or William II.

The Prophet's Strange Omissions

have previously seen the prediction in print or heard it read aloud. Not one person in a thousand possesses so exact a memory as to be able to identify the peculiarities of a text casually listened to or examined a dozen years ago, when there are scores of similar documents with which it might be confused.

Only one point remains which seems to call for notice, and that is the remarkable silence of "Brother Johannes" regarding all those developments of the war which could not have been foreseen in September, 1914. Of the trench fighting and the consequent deadlock of the great armies, of the blockade by submarine, of Germany's cry for food, not a word is said; even Belgium is not so much as mentioned. For us the tragedy of Belgium remains at present the most appalling horror of the war, but on September 10th the tragedy of Belgium had not been consummated. Antwerp was still deemed impregnable, and it must have been before September 10th, probably some time before that date, that Mr. Péladan sent off his manuscript to the editor of the *Figaro*.

I have spent some time over this " prophecy of Brother Johannes," utterly foolish as I consider it to be, simply because it has had so much vogue and because it has been championed by presumably serious people, who do not scruple to maintain that its genuineness is conclusively established by evidence.¹ It only remains to give an illustration of the type of predictions which found favour in the seventeenth century. Both as an example of the tendency to father these extravagant inventions on famous ecclesiastics, and to provide an instance of the figurative use of beasts in political allegory, I may quote an extravagant prophecy, published in the year of the great fire of London, under the name of St. Thomas Becket, the martyred Archbishop of Canterbury. It runs as follows:

The Lily (France) shall remain in the better part, and shall enter into the land of the Lion (Holland), they wanting his assistance, which the beasts of his own kingdom shall tear with their teeth and shall stand in the field among the thorns of his kingdom. At length shall the Son of Man (England) come with a great army, passing the waters, carrying wild beasts in his arms, whose kingdom is in the land of wool, and feared by the whole world. The Eagle (Germany) shall come out of the East with his wings spread upon the sun, with a great multitude of his people to the help of the Son of Man. In that year camps shall be torn, great fear shall be in the world, and in some part of the land of the Lion shall war be amongst many kings, and there shall be a flood of blood. The Lily shall lose his crown with which the Son of Man shall be crowned. And for four following years shall there be many battles amongst

¹ See in particular *The End of the Kaiser*, a brochure by Mr. Ralph Shirley, the editor of the *Occult Review*. The December number of this journal had a label posted on it: "ANTICHRIST AND THE KAISER, THE PROPHECY PROVED GENUINE, BY THE EDITOR."

Allegorical Beasts 65

Christians. Part of the world shall be destroyed; the Head of the World (Pope or Turk) shall be to the earth. The Son of Man and the Eagle shall prevail, and then there shall be peace over the whole face of the earth. Then shall the Son of Man receive a wonderful sign, and shall go into the land of promise.[1]

Extravagant though this may be, it is interesting to note that even in a native English pamphlet " the land of the Lion is used to designate not England but the Netherlands or Flanders, while the animals blazoned on the shield of the King of England are described as 'wild beasts.'" French heralds, indeed, have always called them leopards, and they are so designated in French armorials to this day.[2] It will be understood, therefore, that no objection can be raised against M. Péladan's prophecy on the ground of its identifying England with the Leopard, France with the Cock, or Germany with the Eagle.[3] My contention only is that,

---

[1] *The Prophecies of Thomas Becket, lately found in an ancient Manuscript at Abington by Dr. Ailsworth,* London, 1666. Both the rather incoherent wording and the interpretations in brackets belong to the original pamphlet.

[2] We are told in the *Nouveau Larousse* (1902) " the heraldic leopard is a lion which, instead of being *rampant*, is *passant*, and the head of which faces the spectator," and similarly the authoritative *Dictionnaire archéologique et explicatif de la Science du Blason,* by Comte A. O'Kelly, describes the English royal arms with which we are all familiar as *de gueules, à trois léopards d'or* (gules, three leopards or).

[3] The prophecies, circulated in the sixteenth century under the names of Johann Liechtenberger and Johann Carionis, are full of similar political allegories under the disguise of beasts,

having taken an ancient prediction about Antichrist from no one knows where, he has so modified it and changed its character as to make it say whatever seemed to him desirable.

As a final illustration of the vogue of this kind of allegory among the prophets and prophecy-mongers of the seventeenth century the following passage, which I translate from its Latin original, may also be cited. Curiously enough it comes to us through a certain Johannes (Johannes Wolfius), a Lutheran, who made a prodigious collection of oracles and portents, and who published them in two folio volumes printed in the year 1600. The prophecy itself, however, professes to have been written in 1498.

The Eagle shall fly, and by his flight shall be overthrown the Lion, who will reign at Jerusalem for seven years. At length the princes of Germany will conspire together and the chief men of Bohemia shall be crushed. And the Leopard will devour him. Then a king shall arise of the stock of the eastern Eagle, and there will come the offspring of the Eagle and will build its nest in the house of the Lion, and it will be destitute of all fruit or nourishment from its father. And a king shall be chosen to whom is not paid the honour due to a king. He shall reign, and ruling mightily shall hold sway and will stretch his branches to the uttermost limits of the earth. In his time the Sovereign Pontiff shall be made prisoner and the

etc. We read there of black eagles and young eagles, golden lions and white lions, cocks, wolves, foxes, lilies, etc. But I have not hit upon any which bears a true resemblance in substance to the disclosures of " Brother Johannes."

Black Magic

clergy shall be plundered, for they corrupt the faith. Alas for the evil lives of the clergy!"[1]

The incoherence of these predictions belongs to the original, and is probably intentional. Johannes Wolfius quotes them, as he does many others, with a distinct controversial animus against the Church of Rome.

In taking leave of M. Péladan, the exploiter of this "Brother Johannes" prophecy, it is worth while to notice that he stands charged—amongst others by the late J. K. Huysmans, the author of *En Route*—with engaging in the practice of black magic in a serious and malignant form.[2] I do not propose to discuss here the unpleasant subject of "Satanism," but whether the hideous rites ascribed to the cult are real, or only imaginary, the atmosphere created by these surroundings unquestionably leaves a certain moral stigma attaching to all who allow their names to be prominently associated with it.

[1] Johannes Wolfius, *Lectionum Memorabilium et Reconditarum Centenarii XVI* (Lavingae, 1600), vol. i, p. 722.
[2] See Joanny Bricaud, *J. K. Huysmans et le Satanisme*, Paris, 1913. Huysmans writes: "Il est indiscutable que de Guaita et Péladan pratiquent quotidiennement la magie noire." Bricaud, p. 50, and *cf.* pp. 29 and 37-8.

CHAPTER IV

ARMAGEDDON AND THE END OF WAR

HARDLY any feature is of such common occurrence in the prophecies of all countries and all periods as the prediction of some great conflict of the nations, which generally ends, after terrible sufferings, in the final triumph of religion and justice. These ideas were no doubt largely inspired by the traditional interpretation of Armageddon in the Apocalypse (xvi. 16) as the scene of the ultimate contest between the powers of good and evil. As to the rightfulness of that interpretation this is not the place to inquire, but it permeated all Christian literature and it gave birth to a number of what may be called folk-tales, supposing the word tale to mean simply a thing told and to be capable of referring to the future as well as to the past. There is in particular a whole group of these folk-tales which come from Germany and which, while assuming a good many different forms, centre in an incident commonly known as " the Battle of the Birch Tree "—*die Schlacht am Birkenbaum*. The prophecy is in any case an interesting piece of folk-lore, and I may give it here in what is perhaps its most authentic shape, as it was translated more than sixty years ago in *Blackwood's Magazine.*

A time shall come when the world shall be godless. The people will strive to be independent of king and magistrate, subjects will be unfaithful to their princes. It will then come to a general insurrection when father shall fight against son and son against father. In that time men shall try to pervert the articles of the faith and shall introduce new books. The Catholic religion shall be hard pressed, and men will try with cunning to abolish it. Men shall love play and jest and pleasure of all kinds at that time. But then it shall not be long before a change occurs. A frightful war will break out. On one side shall stand Russia, Sweden, and the whole north, on the other France, Spain, Italy, and the whole south under a powerful prince. This prince shall come from the south. He wears a white coat with buttons all the way down. He has a cross on his breast, rides a grey horse, which he mounts from his left side, because he is lame of one foot. He will bring peace. Great is his severity, for he will put down all dance-music and rich attire. He will hear morning Mass[1] in the church of Bremen. From Bremen he rides to the Haar (an eminence near Werl), from thence he looks with his spy-glass towards the country of the Birch-tree and observes the enemy. Next he rides past Holtum (a village near Werl). At Holtum stands a crucifix between two lime-trees; before this he kneels and prays with

[1] Some copies apparently read, " he will say *(lesen)* Mass."

outstretched arms for some time. Then he leads his soldiers, clad in white, into the battle, and after a bloody contest he remains victorious.

The chief slaughter will take place at a brook which runs from west to east. Woe! woe! to Budberg and Sondern in those days. The victorious leader shall assemble the people after the battle and harangue them in the church.[1]

So runs the best-known version of *die Schlacht am Birkenbaum,* and it is perhaps a little curious that the district which tradition has assigned for the battle-field of this momentous contest is pointed to by military authorities as the scene of the last desperate struggle between Germany and a western invader. So at any rate, says Commander Driant, in his preface to a clever forecast of the war now raging, which was published by M. de Civrieux a couple of years back.[2] The district of Westphalia marked out by the mention of such places as Werl, Holtum, Bremen, Budberg, etc., is about forty miles east of the great Krupp ordinance works at Essen. Still more remarkable at first sight is the fact that the conqueror is to be a man clothed in a white coat with buttons all the way down, who mounts his horse on the wrong

[1] The original German may be found in *Das Buch der Wahr- und Weissagungen* (Regensburg, 1884), pp. 222-3, or again in C. B. Warnefried, *Seherblicke in die Zukunft* (Regensburg, 1861), pt. ii, pp. 59-60. The above translation is taken from *Blackwood's Magazine,* May, 1850, p. 568.

[2] *La Fin de l'Empire allemande—la Bataille du Champ des Bouleaux,* par M. de Civrieux, Paris, 1912.

side. The present Kaiser, as is generally known, owing to an injury at birth, has not the full use of his left arm, and is consequently compelled to climb into the saddle from the off side. Still a moment's consideration of the prophecy shows clearly how trivial the coincidence is. The victorious prince is the leader, not of Germany, but of France and Spain and Italy, a Catholic who hears or even says Mass, and who prays before a crucifix; while the injured limb is not his arm but his foot. Coincidences of this superficial kind must now and again occur in all such predictions, and if we accept them as proof of supernatural insight, there will be no limit to the extravagances into which we shall be led.

Other variants of the prophecy just quoted continued to be repeated until quite modern times. In particular a man named Jaspers, a Westphalian shepherd, of Deininghausen, is said in the year 1830, shortly before his death, to have made a public prediction to this effect:

A great road will be carried through our country from West to East which will pass through the forest of Bodelschwingh. On this road carriages will run without horses and cause a dreadful noise. At the commencement of this work a great scarcity will prevail, pigs will become very dear, and a new religion will arise in which wickedness will be regarded as prudence and good manners. Before this road is quite completed a frightful war will break out.

In 1830 not even the first English railway had been opened, but before 1848 a railway had been constructed in the part of Westphalia spoken of. There was also about this time a great scarcity, and the bringing of workmen into the country led to a deterioration of morals among the peasantry which might have been described as a new religion. All this sounds very promising, but what follows of Jaspers' prophesyings, though vaguely echoing the Birkenbaum predictions, is sadly disappointing when compared with the actual history of the years 1850-70.

1. Before the great road is quite finished a dreadful war will break out.

2. A small northern power will be the conqueror.

3. After this another war will break out, not a religious war among Christians, but between those who believe in Christ and those who do not believe.

4. The war comes from the East; I dread the East.

5. The war will break out very suddenly. In the evening they will say Peace, peace! and yet peace is not; and in the morning the enemy will be at the door. Yet it shall soon pass, and he who knows a good hiding-place, even for only a few days, will be secure.

6. The defeated enemy will have to fly in extreme haste. Let the people cast cart and wheels into the water, otherwise the flying foe will take all vehicles with them.

No disturbance of this kind has certainly taken place in Westphalia from Jaspers' day to

Westphalian Folk Predictions

the present; while on the other hand it must be plain that the circumstances described in no way correspond with anything possible in the war now raging. Prophecies that have missed the mark are almost as uninteresting as a ten-year-old Bradshaw, and if I quote any further details it is only to indicate how little trust can be placed in the precisely similar details which are found in other prophecies. Thus Jaspers declares:

9. The great battle will be fought at the Birch-tree between Unna, Hamm, and Werl. The people of half the world will there stand arrayed against each other. God will terrify the enemy by a dreadful storm. Of the Russians but few shall return home to tell of their defeat.

10. The war will be over in 1850, and in 1852 all will be again in order.[1]

11. The Poles are at first put down; but they will, along with other nations, fight against their oppressors and at last obtain a king of their own.

12. France will be divided internally into three parts.

13. Spain will not join in the war, but the Spaniards shall come after it is over and take possession of the churches.

14. Austria will be fortunate, provided she do not wait too long.

15. The papal chair will be vacant for a time.[2]

---

[1] The article in *Blackwood* from which I borrow this translation was printed in May, 1850, and had probably been written earlier.

[2] *Blackwood's Magazine*, May, 1850, pp. 583-4.

Somewhat more desultory, but even more terrific, are such oracles as the following, extracted from old Westphalian traditions in 1849 by Thomas Beykirch:

Alas! once happy Cologne! when thou art well-paved thou shalt perish in thine own blood. O Cologne! Thou shalt perish like Sodom and Gomorrha; thy stream shall flow with blood and thy relics shall be taken away. Woe to thee, Cologne! because strangers suck thy breasts and the breasts of thy poor—of thy poor who therefore languish in destitution and misery.[1]

Or, again:

Woe! woe! Where Rhine and Moselle meet a battle shall be fought against Turks and Baschkirs (Russians?) so bloody that the Rhine shall be dyed red for twenty-five leagues.[2]

Such predictions as these, however, were no doubt found unsatisfactory for many reasons. It was necessary to bring them up to date and to adapt them to present circumstances if they were to find any general acceptance. We have, I think, a characteristic example of this procedure in a document published by the *Matin* on August 23rd, 1914. It was then described as "The famous Prophecy of Mayence," and was stated to date from 1854, but no indication was given of any book printed in 1854 in which it

[1] This is said to have been found by Heinrich von Juddon in a religious house of the Carmelites.
[2] See Beykirch, *Prophetenstimmen* and *Blackwood*, l.c., p. 567.

could be found, and we may venture to remain sceptical about this fact until more particulars are furnished. As is the case with so many other bogus predictions, the prophecy claims credit for itself on the ground that its earlier forecasts had already been fulfilled with startling exactitude. In the particular instance of this Mayence document verses 5-7 provide a marvellous account of the central incidents of the Franco-Prussian War.

5. Napoleon III at first despising his adversary, will fly very soon towards the "Chesne-Populeux" (near Sedan), where he will disappear never to appear again.

6. In spite of the heroic resistance of the French, a number of soldiers, blue, yellow, and black, will spread themselves over a great part of France.

7. Alsace and Lorraine will be wrested from France for a time and a half.

Certainly if this prophecy of Mayence was really in circulation in 1854, its accuracy as regards these earlier events is very astonishing indeed. The extraordinary thing is that though it had been already famous in 1854 and had been so marvellously verified in 1870, it makes no appearance in any of the elaborate collections of similar materials such as the *Voix Prophétiques* and *Le Grand Pape et le Grand Roi*, the editors of which in 1871 and 1872 scoured heaven and earth in the intervals between their successive editions to add new documents to their store. It seems, then, practically certain that, like so many others, the prophecy of Mayence is a fake, but it is interesting to note how in the nine concluding verses, which presumably have reference to the war now raging, the materials available in the old " Battle of the Birch Tree " saga have been turned to account. I quote the translation published in *The Referee* (August 30th, 1914), which, like many other newspapers, professed to treat the document quite seriously.

10. Courage, faithful souls, the reign of the dark shadow shall not have time to execute all its schemes.

11. But the time of mercy approaches. A prince of the nation is in your midst.

12. It is the man of salvation, the wise, the invincible, he shall count his enterprises by his victories.

13. He shall drive out the enemy of France, he shall march to victory on victory, until the day of divine justice.

14. That day he shall command seven kinds of soldiers against three to the quarter of Bouleaux between Ham, Werl, and Paderborn.

15. Woe to thee, people of the North, thy seventh generation shall answer for all thy crimes. Woe to thee, people of the East, thou shalt spread afar the cries of affliction and innocent blood. Never shall such an army be seen.

16. Three days the sun shall rise upwards on the heads of the combatants without being seen through the clouds of smoke.

17. Then the commander shall get the victory;

Hermann of Lehnin

two of his enemies shall be annihilated, the remainder of the three shall fly towards the extreme East.

18. William, the second of the name, shall be the last King of Prussia. He shall have no other successors save a King of Poland, a King of Hanover, and a King of Saxony.

The seven kinds of soldiers appear to be English, French, Russians, Belgians, Servians, Austrians, and Hungarians. By the "people of the North" Prussia is plainly indicated, by the "people of the East" Austria. It is presumably the Tsar who figures as "the man of salvation," but it would be futile to speculate about the details.

The point of chief interest is the fact that such Westphalian townships as Ham, Werl, and Paderborn are mentioned, and that the translator, being apparently unaware that *bouleau* means a birch-tree, has turned it into a proper name (v. 14). The last verse also apparently betrays adaptation from some older source. Prussia as a separate monarchy is of little interest now. The famous prophecy of Hermann of Lehnin which, while professing to be the work of a mediæval monk, was probably fabricated about 1690, long ago said:

Tandem sceptra gerit, qui stemmatis ultimus erit.

At length he sways the sceptre who will be the last of his race.

But this should properly apply to Frederick William IV, and the defenders of Hermann's prophecy explain it by saying that Frederick William IV. was really the last king of Prussia, for his brother William I, who succeeded him, became Emperor of Germany. By his change of title, they contend, the kingdom of Prussia was virtually extinguished.

Unquestionably the interpreters of the prophets, whether modern or ancient, are driven to hard shifts, and I may state here in concluding that part of our investigation which bears specially on the great war, that of all the utterances which I have examined concerning the results of the contest only two have seemed to suggest even a vague possibility that the prophet possessed intuitions which transcended the limitations of ordinary prudent conjecture. Moreover, the first of these, when traced to its sources, loses all its verisimilitude. Still as it has an interest of its own and recalls some of the features of certain familiar psychic phenomena, it may be recounted here. The narrator is a certain Father Korzeniecki, a Polish Dominican, who, it appears, had a great devotion to the Jesuit martyr Blessed Andrew Bobola, put to death by the Cossacks with most terrible tortures in 1637. The incorrupt body of Blessed Andrew, it should be noted, passed, on the suppression of the Society of Jesus, into the keeping of the Dominicans. One night in the year 1819 Father Korzeniecki, overwhelmed by the tribulations of his beloved Poland, was engaged in prayer to his patron when he saw standing by him a religious in a Jesuit habit, who bade him open his window and look out. Instead of gazing upon the familiar garden of the convent, he beheld a landscape of vast extent stretching as far as the eye could reach. This, he was given to understand by the apparition, was the province of Pinsk in which he, the Blessed Andrew, had suffered martyrdom, and then the Dominican was bidden to look at the prospect again.

At this moment, as the Father viewed the scene a second time, the plain seemed to him suddenly covered with innumerable hordes of Russians, Turks, Frenchmen, Englishmen, Austrians, Prussians, and other nations beside, which the Religious could not exactly distinguish, fighting in a sanguinary hand-to-hand conflict such as might be seen in a war of ruthless extermination. The Father was aghast and bewildered by the horrible spectacle.

"When," said the Martyr, "the war of which you have just seen a picture shall have given way to peace, then Poland shall be restored and I shall be recognized as its principal patron."

It is certainly a curious fact that English and French soldiers should have been given a prominent place in the record of such a dream or vision, and for a moment the coincidence of the Tsar's declaration of liberty for Poland, made at the beginning of the present war, seems rather remarkable. Unfortunately, however, one finds on investigation that the vision first attracted attention at the opening of the Crimean War, and this, I am afraid, offers an only too satisfactory explanation of the fact that Russians, Turks, Frenchmen, and English are named first among the motley armies that were seen in combat on the plains of Pinsk.

The second prophecy is of more importance for the reason that it is not entirely explained by the circumstances under which it was delivered, and that it still, alas! retains a certain intrinsic probability. It is, moreover, a prediction to which, so far as I am aware, no attention has yet been directed. It occurs in a little English Life of a Carmelite nun known as Sister Mary of Jesus Crucified. This Life was privately printed by the late Lady Herbert of Lea in 1887, and the preface was written in the March of that year.[1] It would be no libel upon the undoubted services rendered by Lady Herbert to Catholic religious literature to say that she was not always a conspicuously accurate writer. Nevertheless, this sketch professes on its title-page to be " taken from various documents preserved in the Carmelite monasteries of Pau and Bethlehem," and it certainly shows a considerable dependence on pre-existing materials. It is conceivable, of course, that the author may not have reproduced the data so furnished with entire fidelity, but if she altered them, there seems no assignable reason why she should

---

[1] *A Sketch of the Life of Sister Mary of Jesus Crucified*, by Lady Herbert, London, printed for the author, 1887.

make the good Carmelite say what she does make her say. The general expectation of Catholics at that time did not run in the direction actually followed, but rather the other way. The whole tendency was to anticipate, not to retard, the triumph of the Church. However, let me first set before the reader the two passages which have a bearing on our present subject, only premising that Sister Mary of Jesus Crucified (1846-78) seems to have been a mystic whose religious experiences were altogether startling and abnormal. If we may believe her confessor and her fellow-religious, she not only had constant ecstasies, but she was for several years marked with the stigmata in her hands, feet, and side, from which last wound on every Friday the blood flowed freely. On several occasions she was seen suspended, like St. Joseph a Cupertino, high above the ground, while for many months together, like the Blessed Curé d'Ars and numerous other saints, she is said to have been beaten and tormented by the devil with extraordinary ferocity. With regard, however, to her prophecies, which alone concern us here, the two following passages had better be transcribed exactly as they stand in Lady Herbert's sketch:

One day, while in an ecstasy, she saw a large church in which were many altars. On the principal one was a beautiful rose with a delicious perfume. This she was made to understand represented Pius

IX. Then she saw two kings enter the church with intent to destroy the rose, but they failed. One, however, more bold than the rest, tried to cut it down, but in vain; and he said to himself: "In another year." A little time seemed to elapse, and then she again saw the rose attacked by the two kings, and one of them succeeded in bruising it and tearing off some of the leaves. But afterwards it rose up stronger and more beautiful than before. St. Elias appeared to her and said: "Our present Holy Father is a saint. After him shall come another like no other; he shall suffer much from the hands of his enemies. The third Holy Father shall be the Seraphic. The fourth—alas! alas! there is and shall be no cross like the one he will carry! But the Church will begin to triumph under the rule of this Holy Father, and after his death completely.

Now such manifestations, supposing them to be something more than the mere illusions of a disordered brain, may be assumed to take their colouring from the mystic's previous beliefs and habits of thought. There may sometimes, I hold, be a real intuition of a spiritual truth, even though the setting be fantastic, ridiculous, or contrary to ascertained fact. Joan of Arc, for example, may have been the percipient of perfectly authentic voices though they came to her through a St. Catherine whom she conceived of according to a legend which modern historical criticism has now exploded. The fact that St. Elias' connection with the Carmelites must be considered more than problematical would not

"The Fourth Part of Men" 83

necessarily discredit all the communications of a revelation attributed by a Carmelite nun to his intervention.

But the second passage in this account of Sister Mary's revelations has a more direct bearing on our present subject. After previously speaking of a vision of a dark cloud by which in 1868 the mystic was forewarned of the Franco-Prussian War and the occupation of Rome, the writer continues:

> Later on she seemed to have had a still wider insight into the future. Again she saw the black cloud, very thick, but covering not only France, but the whole of Europe. Then there were fearful wars convulsing every part of Europe; and when they were over, only the fourth part of men remained; the rest had all perished in the struggle. "At that time," she said, "the priests will be few in number, for they will have died for the Faith or in defence of their country. There will be sorrow and mourning everywhere till God's anger is appeased."[1]

Putting these two forecasts together we are left to infer that according to the prophetic intuitions of this strangely favoured mystic, the terrible time of war, thus foretold, was to coincide with the pontificate of the fourth pope of her vision, to wit Benedict XV; for clearly this season of calamity must precede the triumph and peace of the Church which is to begin before the end of his reign, and such an awful visitation as we

[1] *A Sketch of the Life of Sister Mary of Jesus Crucified*, by Lady Herbert (London, 1887), pp. 34 and 36.

are now experiencing would very well explain the words, "Alas! alas! there is and shall be no cross like the one that he will carry."

No exact indication is given of the date of these revelations, but Sister Mary of Jesus Crucified died in August, 1878, six months, that is to say, after the election of Leo XIII and five years before the dream of a great Christian monarchy was shattered for most French Legitimists by the death of the Comte de Chambord. I lay stress on this because if the quotations just given accurately represent the predictions made by Sister Mary, she was not echoing the ideas prevalent among the French religious with whom she lived. As we have already learned from several of the prophecies previously discussed, the whole purport of such publications as the *Voix Prophétiques* and countless others was to encourage the belief that even before the death of Pius IX the Church should see the dawn of a happier age. Necessarily this view was modified after the accession of Leo XIII, but the idea of a comparatively early restoration still persisted. It is recorded of Palma, the *stigmatisée* of Oria, near Brindisi, that shortly before her death she expressed herself in terms which one of the ecclesiastical magnates of the neighbourhood thus reported to Dr. Imbert-Gourbeyre:[1] "She was at one with the other

[1] Imbert-Gourbeyre, *La Stigmatization* (Paris, 1894), vol. i, pp. 568-9.

Defective Evidence

mystics in declaring positively that Pope Leo XIII would not see the triumph of the Church, but, she added, his successor would witness it." Still more noteworthy is Sister Mary's prevision that "fearful wars should convulse every part of Europe" until "only the fourth part of men (? of the male population) remained," and it is certainly curious that she should have foreseen a great dearth of priests, owing in part to the fact that many had died "in defence of their country." There was, so far as I know, no reason in 1878 to suppose that a time would ever come when the clergy would have to take part in battle as combatants.

Nevertheless, the attempt I have been making to find something which can be put forward as a genuine prophecy of these latter times, at once encounters a serious set-back from the fact that in the much fuller and more official Life of Sister Mary of Jesus Crucified, published in 1913,[1] the prediction of universal war and the destruction of three parts of men, apparently finds no place. Moreover, the vision of the Popes is quite differently narrated, though in the larger Life, as in Lady Herbert's sketch, the revelation is communicated to Sister Mary through the prophet St. Elias, and the date of the vision August, 1867, is apparently the same. In the longer Life

[1] *Vie de Sœur Marie de Jésus Crucifié,* par le R. P. Estrate (Paris, Victor Lecoffre, 1913), pp. xviii-408; see especially p. 197.

nothing is said of "the fourth Pope," the present Holy Father. On the contrary, the phrase "there is and shall be no cross like the one he shall carry" (in the French *il n'y aura pas de croix comme celle qu'il aura*) is applied to the successor of Pius IX, *i.e.*, Pope Leo XIII.[1]

Despite these difficulties, the gravity of which I should be sorry to underrate, I am not altogether convinced that the version followed by Lady Herbert is without authority. To begin with, Lady Herbert must have had some text before her, and she can have had no possible object in altering it to suit a much more distant future. Secondly, she was in relation with contemporaries of the ecstatica probably now dead, and we know for certain that an English priest as well as an English nun who had at one time been novice mistress to Sister Mary were among these special sources of information. Thirdly, I think it quite as likely that Père Estrate, the author of the French Life, or those who edited it after his death in 1910, would have felt themselves justified in expurgating or adapting the texts before them (especially in cases where there might be some conflict of evidence), as that Lady Herbert herself would have done so. It might easily have happened, for example, that the idea of priests laying down their lives as

[1] *Vie de Sœur Marie de Jésus Crucifié*, par le R. P. Estrate (Paris), p. 324.

A Prediction verified

combatants in defence of their country might have been considered unseemly by Père Estrate when he first compiled the biography in 1889.

On the other hand one cannot help realizing that the forecast of the four Popes, as Lady Herbert prints it, may have been in part inspired by the prophecy of pseudo-Malachy. The description of the third Pontiff (Pius IX) as the "Seraphic" might very naturally have been suggested by his motto *Ignis ardens* (burning fire), and the use of the phrase *Religio depopulata* (religion laid waste) for Benedict XV unquestionably calls up the idea of a period of suffering and humiliation for the Church and her ruler. Still there is no hint of the beginning of victory either in that motto or in its successor *Fides intrepida*.

Without attempting to decide the point, it seems in any case certain that Sister Mary of Jesus Crucified was regarded by her fellow-religious as endowed with a remarkable gift of prophecy. The fact comes out clearly in a letter which Lady Herbert has preserved, written by the Carmelite Mother Prioress at Bayonne to the English priest above referred to. Towards the end of August, 1870, a colony of nine Carmelite nuns from Pau and Bayonne, the ecstatica Sister Mary of Jesus being one of the number, sailed from Marseilles to establish a house of the Order at Mangalore in India. The letter, which is dated September 2nd, 1870, refers to this rather unusual incident in Carmelite history in the following terms:

You know, dear Father, that I have just sent off three of my dear children to the Indian missions with the Rev. Mother Mary Elias of Pau and five of her daughters, amongst whom is my saintly child Sister Mary of Jesus Crucified. . . . My heart and soul are with my dear children. Sister Elias, my Irish lily, is one of the three; the other two are Sister Mary of the Angels and Sister Mary of St. Joseph. I hope that you have told your good and reverend brother about Sister Mary of Jesus Crucified. You may now do so freely. She is far away now and there is no danger of its doing her any harm. I have been to Pau with my children and have seen and heard many more interesting particulars about her. I will give you another linen steeped in the blood which flowed from her stigmata and which is to perform miracles.[1] She has foretold sad things for some of our Sisters who have sailed, but they are in the hands of God.

This letter, written a few days after the party set sail, confirms the explicit statement of Père Estrate that Sister Mary had foretold that of the nine sisters who went, three would never live to see the new foundation. In point of fact, Sisters Stéphanie and Euphrasie died in the Red Sea

---

[1] The priest in question believed himself, when in the last stage of consumption, to have been miraculously and instantaneously cured by one of these linen cloths. If the original letter was in French the phrase " which is to perform miracles " may represent " qui doit opérer des miracles," which is not quite the same thing.

The Language of Prophecy

and Mother Elias died at Calicut before reaching her intended destination. If we may trust the accuracy of the same French Life several other predictions of the ecstatica concerning domestic events and the future of individuals were fulfilled in an even more remarkable way.

Finally, we shall do well to remember that the language of prophecy is nearly always figurative and grandiose. If He who is the Truth and the Light could describe the repose of His sacred body in the tomb as lasting "three days and three nights" (Matt. xii. 40), we are certainly not constrained to attach an absolutely literal interpretation to such phrases as "the fourth part of men" or "the triumph of the Church." Admitting, as we may do, the bare possibility that the words attributed to the Carmelite ecstatica may have been inspired by some true intuition of the future, we cannot safely infer more than that the conclusion of this terrible war may witness a revival of religious faith and a period of comparative peace for the Church in her unending struggle against principalities and powers.

CHAPTER V

DIVINERS AND SOOTHSAYERS

ON August 31st, 1914, and consequently quite at the beginning of the present war, the following letter appeared in *The Times*. If we may judge by the number of allusions to it which one has come across since, the forecast contained therein must have attracted a good deal of attention.

THE EFFECT OF A PROPHECY.

Sir,—In the summer of 1899 I chanced to be sitting with the present German Secretary for Foreign Affairs, Herr von Jágow (then a Secretary of the German Embassy in Rome), on the balcony of the Embassy, the Palazzo Caffarelli, on the Capitol. In the course of conversation Herr von Jágow expressed the belief that no general European war was likely to occur before the end of 1913. He gave as his reason the influence of a prophecy made to the Kaiser's grandfather, Prince William of Prussia, at Mainz, in 1849. Prince William of Prussia, who was proclaimed German Emperor at Versailles on January 18th, 1871, was in 1849 wandering *incognito* in the Rhine Provinces, attended only by an aide-de-camp. He had incurred great unpopularity by his

Von Jágow's Gipsy Story

attitude during the Berlin revolution of March, 1848, and had been obliged to spend some time in England, whence he returned, still a semi-fugitive, to the Rhineland. At Mainz a gipsy woman offered to tell him his fortune, and addressed him as "Imperial Majesty." Not a little amused—for at that moment his chance of succeeding even to the throne of Prussia seemed slight—the Prince asked, "'Imperial Majesty,' and of what empire, pray?" "Of the new German Empire," was the reply. "And when is this Empire to be formed?" he inquired. The woman took a scrap of paper and wrote on it the year 1849. Then she placed the same figures in column beneath 1849

        1
        8
        4
        9

and adding them together obtained the total 1871
"And how long am I to rule over this Empire?" asked Prince William again. The woman repeated the arithmetical operation, taking the number 1871 and adding the same figures in column . . 1871

        1
        8
        7
        1

which gave the result 1888
    Astonished by her confidence, the Prince then asked, "And how long is this fine Empire to last?" Then the woman, taking

the figures 1888 and repeating the same
operation 1888
                                      1
                                      8
                                      8
                                      8
                                    ─────
obtained the result 1913

The story soon spread in Prussian Court circles. Prince William became German Emperor in 1871 and died in 1888. The effect of the double fulfilment of the prophecy upon the present German Emperor's mind was great, and, as my experience shows, it entered into the calculation of Prussian diplomatists as long ago as 1899. May we not have here a psychological clue to the failure of the German Emperor to use his influence for peace during the diplomatic negotiations of last month?—I am, Sir, yours,   VIDI.

Although the year 1913 is undoubtedly past beyond recall, the lovers of mystery are loth to allow so promising an example of what they call cabbalistic divination to fizzle out like an exploded squib. The year 1913, they contend, may still be regarded as fatal because it was the last year of the Kaiser's unchallenged supremacy. It does not seem to occur to them that by this lax interpretation they are multiplying the mathematical chance by three, for if the empire had been overthrown in 1912 the same interpreters would undoubtedly have urged that the prophecy was verified, on the ground that

Variants of the Story 93

the year 1913 stood first in the new order of things. In point of fact, even as an historical incident, the story abounds in suspicious features. To begin with, it is told in several different ways. For example, a French brochure, *Prédictions sur la Fin de l'Allemagne,* which is followed by Mr. W. M. Fullerton in a book recently published, *Problems of Power,*[1] refers to it as the " prediction of Fiensberg "—Fiensberg being, it seems, a village near Baden where the incident occurred. According to this version a certain Countess R., who was supposed to be gifted with second sight, had been asked by William, then Prince of Prussia, what she could tell him about his future destiny. In answer the Countess simply took him through the little series of addition sums which has just been given. On the other hand, according to Mr. F. L. Rawson,[2] a Paris variant declares that the prophet lived in England and was a thought-reader by profession, but as the future Emperor visited England in 1848, and not in 1849, the amendment seems eminently improbable. Another account[3] states that the Emperor William I consulted a clairvoyante when he was a young man as far back as 1829. She bade him add up the digits ($1829 + 1 + 8 + 2 + 9 = 1849$) and told him

---

[1] Fullerton, *Problems of Power* (London, 1913), p. 282, note.
[2] F. L. Rawson, *How the War will end* (London, 1914), p. 46. This writer also refers to a version in the *Neue Metaphysische Rundschau,* January, 1912.
[3] See *Light,* February 24th, 1912.

his life would be attempted in 1849, and the rest as before. In any case, we may assert with confidence that neither the gipsy woman, nor the Countess R., nor anyone else in 1849, invented this very innocent arithmetical device for guessing at the future. The method is abundantly illustrated in a book published in 1842, called *Amusements Philologiques,* by "G. P. Philomneste," of which there were also earlier editions. In this little work the following remarkable example is given, not as connected with any story of successful divination but simply as an arithmetical curiosity:

Robespierre fell and the Reign of Terror ended in 1794, adding the sum of these digits to the date we get: $1794+1+7+9+4=1815$, which is the year of the fall of Napoleon. Again pursuing the same process a stage further, we obtain $1815+1+8+1+5=1830$, which saw the fall of Charles X and with him of the Bourbon dynasty. Thus:

1794	1815
1	1
7	8
9	1
4	5
1815	1830
(Battle of Waterloo)	(Expulsion of the Bourbons)

Napoleon III's Fatal Year

Perhaps almost the only example which can be quoted of a prophecy which is extant, in black and white, at a date earlier than the time of its verification, is a numerical prognostic of the same kind which may be found in *Notes and Queries* for September 15th, 1866, p. 215:

Louis Napoleon, says the writer, was proclaimed Emperor (see *Hartland's Tables*) in January, 1853. Add to this year the digits either of this date, or of his birth (in 1808), or of the birth of the Empress Eugénie (in 1826), and we get:

$$\text{Became Emperor Empire} \begin{cases} 1853 \\ 1 \\ 8 \\ 5 \\ 3 \end{cases} \quad \text{Birth} \begin{cases} 1853 \\ 1 \\ 8 \\ 0 \\ 8 \end{cases} \quad \begin{matrix} \text{Birth} \\ \text{of} \\ \text{Empress} \end{matrix} \begin{cases} 1853 \\ 1 \\ 8 \\ 2 \\ 6 \end{cases}$$

$$\overline{1870} \quad \overline{1870} \quad \overline{1870}$$

And, indeed, we might join to these converging coincidences the results given by the date of Louis Napoleon's marriage with the Empress, which also took place in 1853. But this very prognostic, which looks so startling when we find it set out in print four years before the battle of Sedan, *i.e.*, before the downfall of the second Empire, also illustrates in a remarkable way how purely fortuitous is the significance of the whole computation. In point of fact Napoleon was not proclaimed Emperor in January, 1853, but in December, 1852. It is true, as the writer in *Notes and Queries* states, that the date

96   Diviners and Soothsayers

assigned in Hartland's *Chronological Dictionary* is January, 1853, but this is simply a blunder. A hundred different authorities could be quoted to show that the second Empire began in the preceding year. Moreover, we have only to select our facts a little differently and it is easy to prove, this time without the aid of any erroneous chronology, that the *annus fatalis* for Louis Napoleon ought to have been 1869, not 1870. The revolution, which ended in Napoleon being elected President of the Republic, was in 1848. Add 1+8+4+8 to 1848 and we get 1869. Again, he became Emperor in 1852, he was born in 1808, Eugénie was born in 1826, and they were married in 1853. From all these we obtain the date 1869, as the following figures show:

$$\text{Emperor} \begin{cases} 1852 \\ 1 \\ 8 \\ 0 \\ 8 \end{cases} = 1869 \qquad \text{Empress Born} \begin{cases} 1852 \\ 1 \\ 8 \\ 2 \\ 6 \end{cases} = 1869 \qquad \text{Married} \begin{cases} 1852 \\ 1 \\ 8 \\ 5 \\ 3 \end{cases} = 1869$$

This agreement is curious, but not so very remarkable. A really surprising coincidence, however, is revealed when we apply the same treatment to the case of Louis Philippe, the immediate predecessor of Napoleon as ruler of France. Louis Philippe became king in 1830; he was born in 1773, his queen was born in 1782, and he was married in 1809. Now this gives us:

Date of Accession:	1830	Date of wife's birth	1830	Date of marriage	1830
Date of birth	1 7 7 3		1 7 8 2		1 8 0 9
	1848		1848		1848

Strange to say, 1848 was, in fact, the date of Louis Philippe's downfall. But, in spite of a similar unanimity of the prognostics, it was in 1870, and not in 1869, that the overthrow of Napoleon actually came to pass.

The fact is, that when one takes the trouble to look into it, the mystery admits of a very simple explanation. The sum of the digits of any modern date must in any case lie between 9 and 27, most commonly between 15 and 25. Now an interval of from 15 to 25 years is the sort of period in which momentous political changes come about, and if one selects one's starting-point judiciously it is not difficult to hit upon coincidences. Take, for example, the election of Pope Leo XIII in 1878. Add these digits together and you have $1878+1+8+7+8=1902$ for the election of his successor, and the sum of the digits of this last date ($1902+1+9+2=1914$) would prepare us for the coming of another new Pope in 1914. As a matter of fact, Pope Leo XIII was inconsiderate enough to upset our calculation by dying in 1903 instead of in 1902, but the forecast might have been claimed by any

98 Diviners and Soothsayers

aspirant to seership as a very near thing, and he might plead in extenuation of this slight miscarriage of his previsions, that in any case Pope Pius X must have been fated to die in 1914 because the most conspicuous epoch in his career was 1893, in which year he was both created Cardinal and named Patriarch of Venice, and $1893+1+8+9+3=1914$, the year of his death.

It was suggested above that to secure successful divination upon these lines it is essential to choose one's starting point judiciously. For example, any embryo Zadkiel who chanced to notice that the date of the accession of the unfortunate Louis XVI, *i.e.*, 1774, contained a premonition of the time of his execution upon the scaffold ($1774+1+7+7+4=1793$) would be careful not to proclaim this fact baldly in such a way that it seemed a mere isolated coincidence. He would probably invent a picturesque setting for his prognostic and develop it as far as possible; something, for example, in this style.

It was the year 1760, at the crisis of the struggle between the Encyclopédistes and the Jesuits. The Encyclopédistes stood for the new godless philosophy of Voltaire, and the Jesuits, so soon to be expelled from France, represented clericalism and the *ancien régime*. To an aged Jesuit, filled with sadness at the political outlook, there came the *gouvernante* of the little Prince Louis, son of the Dauphin and grandson

King Louis XVI

of the King. She asked the good priest why he seemed so sad, what misfortune threatened.

"I have been studying," he replied, "the cabbalistic properties of numbers, and what I see fills me with alarm. Add up the digits of the present year, 1760. One and seven and six and nought."

"That makes 14, Father."

"Well, in 14 years' time, that is in 1774, this little prince, still a mere boy, will be called upon to govern France. But further add up for me the digits of 1774."

"The sum, Reverend Father, is 19."

"And if you add 19 to 1774 what do you get then?"

"It gives us 1793."

"Then I would have you know that in 1793 this poor boy will perish by a most terrible death, and that with him will fall the whole political order which he represents."

"Is that the end?"

"No; sum up yet again the digits of 1793, and add this also to the year itself."

"That, Father, will bring us to 1813."

"Well, in 1813 a battle will be fought which will place France at the mercy of the other nations of Europe. The empire founded by a tyrant on the ruins of our kingship will then, in its turn, be overthrown."

Of course it would have been more effective if

we could have come out at the year 1815, the Battle of Waterloo; but the Battle of Leipzig in 1813 does very well, and it was really the end of the Napoleonic usurpation. This, in any case, is a more impressive presentment of the facts than the statement of a single coincidence, and it is all due to the prudent selection of 1760 as a starting-point. You take 1760 because the digits happen to bring you to the 1774, which you want, and no other year would serve. The same principle, if I mistake not, has guided the choice of the year 1849 for the starting-point of the Kaiser Wilhelm prognostic. Nothing momentous happened to the Prince of Prussia in 1849. He did not come to the throne in that year, or attain any new dignity, but the sum of the digits of 1849, when added to the date itself, happens to yield 1871; 1871, similarly treated, conducts you to 1888, which is really the only coincidence in the series; 1888, with its digits added, comes very near to landing us in the great European cataclysm now going on around us, but, as usual, spoils the sequence by being just a year or two out, in this case a year or two too early.

It may be worth while to add that some arithmetical prognostic of the kind here discussed seems to have been current in Germany as early as 1882, that is to say, six years before the death of Kaiser Wilhelm I. But Miss Max Wall's letter on the subject to *Light* (August 22nd,

An Arithmetical Prognostic

1914) does not leave a very clear impression of the nature of the prophecy which was then in circulation. In any case no one has so far produced any reliable evidence to show that the prediction had been heard of before the period of the Franco-Prussian War.

It is plain then that no reliance can be placed on this method of arithmetical divination. The instances in which it seems occasionally to be verified are mere coincidences. Neither can such coincidences be regarded as at all extraordinary, seeing that the mathematical chance against their occurrence cannot ordinarily be rated higher than at about 20 to 1. Moreover, it will hardly be disputed that the whole process is puerile and arbitrary in the highest degree. Perhaps this last aspect of the matter may best be emphasized by a sort of *reductio ad absurdum*. Here is an arithmetical computation made in one of those prophecy books previously spoken of, in which pious Legitimists, after the close of the Franco-Prussian war, sought confirmation for the belief they professed in the speedy triumph of Henri V and Pius IX. Could anything be more pathetic than the state of mind which finds comfort in such reasoning as the following?:

The Venerable Anna Maria Taigi predicted that Pius IX would reign twenty-seven years and about six months, and that he would consequenetly die in the 28th year of his pontificate.

A very curious cabbalistic calculation leads us to

the same result. Take first the signature of the Holy Father *Pius Papa nonus* (Pius IX Pope), and secondly his motto in the prophecy of St. Malachy *Crux de Cruce*. Make a Latin alphabet (since the words which we are now concerned with are Latin words) and number it. There are 23 letters, as you know, since i and j only count as one letter, and similarly u and v, and there is no w. Then a counts 1, b 2, c 3, and so on until we get to $z=23$. Then make your first trial; take the signature. *Pius* gives you 62; *Papa* 32; *nonus* 78. Add these cabbalistically and you have $6+2+3+2+7+8=28$. Treat the motto in the same way. *Crux* gives 61; *de* 9; *cruce* 48. Once more add these together cabbalistically and you have $6+1+9+4+8=28$. A Jewish cabbalist would at once draw the inference that *Pius Papa nonus* is identical with the personage designated by *Crux de Cruce*, since they both yield the same number.[1]

The worthy Abbé Chabauty, who is the author of this marvellous rigmarole, proceeds to push his conclusions even further; but we will be content to note that after these developments he

---

[1] *Lettres sur les prophéties modernes et Concordance de toutes les Prédictions* (Paris, 1872), p. 155.

This device of attaching a numerical value to the letters of our alphabet is not entirely unknown in England. Let me quote the following illustration from *The Principles of Science* of W. S. Jevons, 3rd ed., p. 263. He gives it as an example of a curious coincidence:

"The French Chamber of Deputies in 1830 consisted of 402 members, of whom 221 formed the party called 'La queue de Robespierre,' while the remainder, 181 in number, were named 'Les honnêtes gens.' If we give to each letter a numerical value corresponding to its place in the alphabet it will be found that the sum of the values of the letters in each name exactly indicates the number of the party."

comes back with much satisfaction to the main point, viz., that the pontificate of twenty-eight years thus assigned to Pius X is not only in exact accord with the prophecy of Anna Maria Taigi, but also with the "three years and a little longer" assigned by Marie Lataste for the desolation of Rome. In August, 1870, Rome was left defenceless when Napoleon withdrew the French troops from the city. The three years would be up in August, 1873, the Pope, according to Anna Maria Taigi's prophecy of a pontificate of $27\frac{1}{2}$ years, would die about the middle of December, 1873, and consequently between September, 1873, and the December of the same year, Catholics would see the patrimony of the Holy See restored. The complete triumph of the Church, however, would only come when, after the death of Pius IX, the victorious monarch of France, Henri V, should instal the Pope's successor upon the chair of St. Peter with every circumstance of pomp and splendour.

So M. Abbé Chabauty dreamed in 1871. I do not know how many editions his book went through. The copy I have before me is of the second edition, issued by a first rate firm of religious publishers in Paris in 1872.[1] Such speculations do not call for much discussion when we look back upon them forty years after-

[1] The book indeed bears the imprint both of Henri Oudin of Poitiers and Victor Palmé of Paris. The latter firm issued the reprint of the Bollandist *Acta Sanctorum* in 60 vols. folio, as well as numberless other important works.

wards. It is sufficient to remind the reader that Pope Pius IX died not in 1873 but in 1878, still virtually a prisoner, that to this day the temporal authority of the Holy See does not extend beyond the precincts of the Vatican, and that the Comte de Chambord (Henri V) ended in 1883 a life which had almost entirely been spent in exile from his native land.

Quite apart from any pretence of the quasi-scientific manipulation of numbers there exists at all times a literature of divination, the extent of which is realized by few who have not personally made acquaintance with it. For the one or two publications like Old Moore's Almanack and Zadkiel's Almanack, of which the names are familiar to the general reader, there are scores of others in every European language which equally profess to unveil the future and which are invariably more or less identified with the jargon of astrology and horoscopy. Beyond a few passing words I have no intention of attempting to deal with the subject here, but it seems worth while to point out, however briefly, that the true cause of the favour shown to these bogus prophecies lies in the disposition of the uncritical mind to count only the successes and persistently to ignore the failures. As Bacon says in his essay on the subject, "Men marke when they hit, and never marke when they misse." The tendency is by no means confined to persons of a conspicuously religious temperament. Quite recently the strong impression made upon an acquaintance of a very opposite habit of mind—the incarnation, I should have judged of robust scepticism—by the vaticinations of the celebrated Mr. Zadkiel concerning the present war, induced me to make an investigation both of this and of some copies of the Almanack published under the name of "Old Moore." The inquiry, I confess, when not confined to one issue but extending over several years, proved distinctly interesting as a revelation of the methods followed by the compilers of this class of publications. But let me quote first the prognostics which had excited the alarm of my usually incredulous friend. In connection with the total eclipse of the sun which took place on August 21st, 1914, Zadkiel nine months before had remarked:

Junctinus averred that a great eclipse of the sun in Leo "presignifies the motion of armies, death of a king, danger of war, and scarcity of rain." In countries and cities ruled by the sign Leo such events would be most likely to take place—in France, Italy, Sicily, Roumania, Rome, etc. As the eclipse falls in opposition to the place of the moon at the birth of the King of Italy, his Majesty should as far as possible avoid war and safeguard his health this year and for the next two years.

It is singular that this great eclipse falls in the exact place of Mars in the summer solstice. The rulers of Prussia and Austria should accept the warning also.

Taken thus far, the seer's forecast might easily impress the casual reader as evincing a somewhat uncanny insight into future events. But it goes on:

At St. Petersburg Mars is only two degrees past the mid-heaven, and Venus is in the tenth house, so that the influences are well balanced as to peace and strife, and accordingly there is ground for hope that Europe will be spared a great war and that the great nations, if not all, will be enabled to pursue their peaceful occupations.

Here we have, of course, an obvious inclination to hedge, but even with this qualification it is quite intelligible that anyone who did not know Mr. Zadkiel and his ways should credit him with a rather remarkable hit. It is only when we come to look at the previous issues, and note that the complications of the Eastern question and the growing armaments of Germany have induced our astrologers to persist year after year in prophesying war that we appreciate how little it all amounts to. Thus for the politically peaceful autumn of 1911 Zadkiel issued the warning:

Mars flames fiercely close to the mid-heaven. This should be a serious warning to our Government to strengthen army and navy and to keep a sharp eye on the North Sea and the East of Europe and Egypt. The ancient aphorism relating to such a configuration indicates "quarrels, discords, and bloodshed." Should peace in Europe and Asia be happily secured, then there is a risk that political

War in 1912!

strife will culminate in discords, strikes, and serious riots in England, Wales, and Ireland.

This was no doubt the autumn of the railway strike, but disturbances thus vaguely indicated and safeguarded are a very safe card to play. For the spring of 1912 (which, except for the Italo-Turkish War, begun in the previous September, passed away peacefully and uneventfully), we have the following startling announcement in capitals:

As the central line of the solar eclipse passes, etc. . . . the danger of WAR IN EUROPE is imminent, and it is our duty to warn the rulers of European countries of this danger. . . . It is imperative that England should strengthen army and navy and prepare to meet sudden attack by a formidable combination on her great empire.

In May, 1912, we have this caution from the same source:

A most critical time is at hand in the United Kingdom, in Europe, and in the United States, and it will be a matter for great thankfulness if bloodshed and warfare can be avoided and if the breakers of solemn treaties and the instigators of piratical warfare can be compelled to keep the peace. . . . The 10th and 21st and the last few days seem to be the most critical for the civilized world, especially for Russia, Prussia, and France.

This might have served very well for a forecast of August, 1914, but it had not a shadow of justification in May, 1912. It would be absurd to multiply further illustrations. Let me only notice that for the same year, 1914, side by side with the relatively well-founded caution against war, we have such wild shots as the following:

August, 1914. Our relations with Russia appear to be strained. It is to be hoped that the threatened rupture may be averted. . . . Towards the close of the month there may again be trouble in Bengal. In and around Delhi the Viceroy should be well guarded.

Or, again:

September, 1914. About the 7th of the month there are indications of female influence being adverse to Parliamentary proceedings, and it is possible that the suffragists will become obstreperous.

Similarly in 1913 Zadkiel announced:

This seems to presignify that the Liberal Government will become very unpopular and meet with a speedy overthrow.

There can be little doubt—and a comparison of the issues for successive years strongly deepens the impression—that the prophetic utterances of Zadkiel and Old Moore are carefully calculated, in accordance with what seems to be the balance of probabilities, to score as many hits as possible. An immense number of shots are made—that many of them are mutually inconsistent matters little—and it is hoped that a fair proportion of these will go near enough to the mark to be claimed as successes. This multiplication of predictions is in many of these books reduced to a system by making the prognostics three times over—first in the calendar itself, then in a general summary of the prophetic outlook, and lastly by separately calculating the horoscope of all prominent political personages. In each of these divisions new forecasts are introduced and they are often quite divergent from each other in tone, sometimes absolutely irreconcilable. On the other hand, nearly all statements are qualified and safeguarded. We are not told positively that a war will take place, but that peace is seriously menaced; we are not informed that the Emperor of Austria, for example, will die, but that he ought to take care of his health. If any calamity of the kind hinted at actually occurs the prophet claims a success and duly advertises it in next year's issue. If nothing happens the catastrophe is supposed to have been providentially averted and the prediction attracts no further attention—at any rate, it is not counted as a failure. Even when successes are proclaimed with an immense flourish of trumpets those readers who will take the trouble to compare the events as they actually occur with the wording of the forecast will almost invariably find that the data calculated to mislead are far in excess of the details that are verified. For example, in the *Antares Almanac* for 1913 an announcement was made concerning the Kaiser, which has been much quoted as a most wonderful example of astrological divination. The whole passage runs as follows :

Diviners and Soothsayers

THE GERMAN EMPEROR WILLIAM II.

The Kaiser's star courses in 1913 and 1914 are brooding. They are a menace both to his health and fortunes, but chiefly to his fortunes. Such aspects as these will, we fear, impel him to declare war either against England or France in 1913 or 1914, and these aspects threaten him with heavy money loss. Disaster, therefore, will attend his military operations. Verily, the stars will be fighting against the German Emperor as they fought against Sisera of old, but it is especially on the sea that disaster will overtake him. We have no hesitation in predicting the destruction of the whole of the German fleet if, as we expect, Germany engages herself in war with England; for our King's star courses are propitious and indicate success, whilst the Kaiser's indicate unmitigated disaster. We regard 1913 and 1914 as the most critical and perilous years of the Kaiser's life, both for his health and fortunes. They are years not only of aggressive fortune, but of the malice of fortune.

Now to begin with, the prophet, we notice, gives himself a margin of two years. This seems to me a generous allowance, when, after all, in predicting war, he was only echoing the confident anticipations of two-thirds of our journalists. Then he certainly implies that by the end of 1914 catastrophe will have overtaken the Kaiser, that his fleet will have been annihilated, or that, in any case, disaster at sea will be the outstanding feature of any hostilities which are set on foot. Nothing is said of the conquest of

Belgium, of the occupation of a considerable slice of French territory, of a campaign successfully maintained against the numerical preponderance of Russia. It is true that the final issue has not yet been reached. Overthrow and financial ruin may still be the ultimate fate of the aggressor, but any rash believer who allowed himself to be guided in, let us say, his commercial speculations, by this exceptionally "successful" forecast of the Antares seer, would almost certainly have laid up for himself a time of bitter disappointment, if not of irretrievable disaster. And if this is the case with the successes, what is to be said of the failures?

I am not now expressing any opinion as to the abstract possibility of foretelling the future. One hears wonderful stories of the predictions made by palmists and others. It would not be scientific to assert *a priori* that all these stories must be untrue. Even though we can give no rational explanation of the phenomena of second sight, it would be rash to declare it to be a myth. But so far as I have had any opportunity of testing such accounts, I have never yet met with a satisfactory example of an event *of public interest* which had been clearly foretold by any palmist or clairvoyante. There are always flaws, and generally serious flaws, in the evidence by which such stories of successful divination are substantiated. Whenever a great crisis—say, for example, an Arctic expedition—is expected, there are a thousand reasons why any soothsayer who is conscious of possessing the power to foresee the result should exercise that gift. There are equally a thousand reasons which would prompt him or her to have the prediction put on record, in the clearest terms and with the strictest formalities, while yet that result is unknown. But though there are innumerable prophecies made and even printed, it is still possible for serious students of psychic phenomena to debate whether all history can show a single reliable instance of the prevision of an unguessable future event, especially, as said above, an event of public interest.

The palmist "Madame de Thèbes" has the reputation of having foretold the terrible conflagration at the "Bazar de la Charité" in which the Duchesse d'Alençon and so many other great ladies lost their lives. Unfortunately no adequate evidence establishes the genuineness of the prediction. If the claim were indisputable, it would be greatly to the pecuniary interest of Mme. de Thèbes to put the evidence for the prophecy permanently on record. Most of our palmists and diviners do not disdain to receive money for the exercise of their peculiar faculty.[1]

---

[1] I am not in the least disputing the power possessed by many persons of unveiling the past secret history and present difficulties of those (often complete strangers) who come to consult them. Of that gift more than one explanation may be offered. But the question now before us concerns only the knowledge of the future.

It is curious that they should be content to receive guineas and half-guineas for regulating the love affairs of quite obscure people, when an assured knowledge of the approach of war, the spread of revolution, and the death of monarchs and statesmen, would make such gifted persons the very kings of the Stock Exchange if they directed their energies to a more remunerative field of industry. What financier was it who said that he did not ask to know the future twelve months ahead, but that if any lady could always tell him what was going to happen the day after to-morrow he would be delighted to offer her a retaining fee of fifty thousand a year for her exclusive services?

Consequently when the same Mme. de Thèbes chimes in with the Antares prophet and tells us with much eloquence and *entrain* all kinds of gruesome things about the Kaiser's horoscope, I confess she leaves me unmoved. Here is a specimen culled from the *Almanach de Mme. de Thèbes* for 1913:

Germany menaces Europe in general and France in particular. When the war breaks out she will have willed it, but after it there will be no longer Hohenzollern or Prussian domination. I have said, and I repeat, that the days of the Emperor are numbered, and after him all will be changed in Germany—I say his days of reign, I do not say his days of life.

In the Almanac for 1914 she continues in the

same strain, but it would serve no good purpose to quote further.

I do not deny that curious coincidences occasionally take place. Even when we have eliminated the mystifications caused by the supplementary matter imported at a much later date into the original Centuries of Nostradamus, it must seem a rather astonishing fact that two of the most tragic incidents of the history of England in the seventeenth century should have been announced in Paris nearly a hundred years before they happened.[1] Whatever the obscurities of the context, obscurities that are met with in every quatrain attributed to Nostradamus, the words *Senat de Londres mettront à mort leur Roi* can admit of but one interpretation. But it may be interesting to quote the whole quatrain, together with an early English translation:

> Gand et Bruceles marcheront contre Anvers,
> Senat de Londres mettront à mort leur Roi;
> Le sel et vin luy seront à l'envers
> Pour eux avoir le regne en desarroy.
> —(*Cent.* IX, 49.)

> Brussels and Ghent 'gainst Antwerp forces bring,
> And London's Senate put to death their King;

---

[1] Klinckowstroem in his essay *Die ältesten Ausgaben der Prophéties des Nostradamus* has carefully examined into the dates and contents of the early editions. It is sufficient for my present purpose to note that all the prophecies of special interest to English readers are to be found in print in editions earlier than 1605. Most of them are much older, for Michel Nostradamus himself died in 1566.

The Salt and Wine not able to prevent
That warlike Kingdom's universal rent.

Here, also, is the quatrain which is supposed to predict the Fire of London, with its date, 1666:

Le sang du juste à Londres fera faute
Bruslez par foudres de vingt trois les six;
La dame antique cherra de place haute,
De mesme secte plusieurs seront occis.
—(*Cent.* II, 51.)

The blood o' the just London rues full sore
When to thrice twenty, you shall add six more,
The ancient Dame shall fall from her high place,
And the like mischief others shall deface.

Whether Ghent and Brussels can in any sense be said to have marched to Antwerp towards the close of the Thirty Years' War, whether "salt and wine" can stand for France or have any intelligible meaning at all, whether *de vingt trois les six* can represent 1666, whether *la dame antique* is to be identified with St. Paul's Cathedral, and so forth, are questions which cannot be discussed here. In any case, it is probably sufficient to say that no clever charlatan who chooses to throw all order and consistency to the winds, and who sketches in cryptic language an infinity of possible future occurrences, can fail to score some hits in the course of more than three centuries. The brilliant epigram, whether it was Beza's or another's, which represents Nostradamus as the prince of humbugs, probably comes nearer to the truth than anything that was ever said of him by his admirers:

> Nostra damus cum falsa damus nam fallere nostrum est,
> Et cum falsa damus, nil nisi nostra damus.[1]

As for the other more famous predictions of public occurrences, they have for the most part been deliberate fabrications concocted after the event. Such, for example, is the well-known prophetic vision of the horrors of the French Revolution, attributed to Cazotte, the author of *Le Diable amoureux*. No one now seriously doubts that the whole was a hoax or *jeu d'esprit* of which La Harpe was the true author. On the other hand, Döllinger is satisfied of the truth of the statement that, thirteen years before the outbreak of the Revolution, a celebrated preacher, Beauregard, declared from the pulpit of Notre Dame:

> The temples of God will be plundered and destroyed, His festivals abolished, His name blasphemed, His service proscribed. Yea, what hear I? What see I? In place of hymns in praise of God, loud and profane songs will be sung here, and the heathen goddess Venus herself will dare here to take the place of the living God, to set herself on the altar and to reeive the homage of her true worshippers.[2]

---

[1] The epigram, which turns on a pun, for Nostradamus means in Latin "we give our own," is quite untranslatable. It means literally "we give our own when we give you lies, for lying is our trade; and when we give you lies we give you nothing but our own."

[2] Döllinger, *Prophecies and the Prophetic Spirit*, p. 16.

But this Döllinger justly considers not to exceed the limits of natural prevision in a man thoroughly well acquainted with the moral corruption and blasphemous spirit of the times.

Of faked modern predictions an example of a quite different purport may be quoted from a booklet which a few years ago professed to record the prophecies of "Mother Shipton." Mother Shipton herself, according to Sir Sidney Lee,[1] is probably a mythical personage, but she is supposed to have foretold all kinds of historical events, and amongst other things that Cardinal Wolsey, though Archbishop of York, should never visit his cathedral city. She was also said to have predicted the Civil Wars and the Fire of London. But a volume printed in 1872 went still further and attributed to her the following:

ANCIENT PREDICTION.

Entitled by popular tradition "Mother Shipton's Prophecy"; published in 1448, republished in 1641.

Carriages without horses shall go,
And accidents fill the world with woe.
Around the world thoughts shall fly,
In the twinkling of an eye.
The world upside down shall be,
And gold be found at the root of tree.
Through hills man shall ride
And no harm be at his side.
Under water men shall walk,
Shall ride, shall sleep, shall talk.

[1] *Dict. of Nat. Biogr.*, s.v.

In the air men shall be seen,
In white, in black, in green.
Iron in the water shall float
As easily as a wooden boat.
Gold shall be found and shown
In a land that's now not known.
Fire and water shall wonders do
England at last shall admit a foe.
The world to an end shall come
In eighteen hundred and eighty-one.[1]

As the language alone would suffice to show, the whole was a modern fake, and a Mr. Charles Hindley subsequently admitted that he had fabricated it.

I will conclude with a reference to the one single instance I have ever come across in which an event which could be called an event of public interest seems to have been really foretold before it came to pass. It is quoted, with what appear to be exact references, in the *Annales des Sciences Psychiques*,[2] though the prophecy after all does not amount to very much.

At the beginning of June, 1905, a certain Scandinavian merchant, a Mr. Thorlakur O. Johnson, had a vision of the death by an accident of the reigning King Frederick VIII of Denmark, and it was in some way conveyed to him that this would take place in 1912. He narrated the vision next day to a friend, a Mr.

[1] See *Notes and Queries*, December 7th, 1872, p. 450; also April 26th, 1873.
[2] *Annales des Sciences Psychiques*, August, 1912, pp. 250-1.

A Public Event foretold

Thorkell Thorlaksson, and induced the latter to make a formal record of it in these terms: "King Frederick VIII will die in the course of 1912 as the result of an accident." Mr. Johnson seems also to have mentioned the vision to several other persons, amongst the rest to Mr. G. T. Zoega, a well-known scholar, author of an Icelandic dictionary published by the Clarendon Press. The fact is curious, and it seems well authenticated, but it may be doubted whether this fulfilment of what seems to have been no more than an exceptionally vivid dream can be considered to lie outside the range of mere accidental coincidence. Most assuredly we should have heard nothing of the matter if the prediction had not been fulfilled.

CHAPTER VI

THE SO-CALLED PROPHECY OF ST. MALACHY

IN the course of the preceding chapters reference has many times been made to certain mottoes attached to the Popes of these latter times. Almost every reader is aware that the phrase *crux de cruce* (cross from a cross) is identified with Pius IX, that *lumen in cœlo* (light in the heavens) belongs to Leo XIII, that Pius X and his present Holiness, Benedict XV, are respectively characterized as *ignis ardens* (burning fire) and *religio depopulata* (religion laid waste). Mottoes such as these and such as those also which await the two next Popes, to wit, *fides intrepida* (undaunted faith) and *pastor angelicus* (the angelic shepherd), can cause no misgiving in the mind of the simple-hearted believer. He likes to think them divinely bestowed, and he knows of no special reason why they should be pronounced inappropriate. Tradition seems to be in their favour, and they are so commonly taken for granted that the plain man is prompted to conclude that if there was any flaw, so to speak, in their original title to rank as prophetic utterances, the flaw has been made good by subsequent ratification or by what canonists would call a *sanatio in radice*. This is no doubt a very natural attitude of mind and a belief in itself quite harmless. None the less, it is certainly illogical, and the perverse use which has been made of these mottoes to bolster up predictions of quite a different order renders it desirable that the fraudulent and ignoble origin of this pretended prophecy should be more generally understood than it is.[1]

The oracular utterances of which we speak form part of a long series of similar mottoes which is supposed to have been delivered in the spirit of prophecy by St. Malachy, an Irish Cistercian monk, who became Archbishop of Armagh. St. Malachy lived in the twelfth century, and was the friend of St. Bernard, who wrote a short life of him. The great founder of Clairvaux informs us very casually that "the gift of prophecy was not denied" to the saintly Archbishop,[2] but with the exception of this brief

[1] As an illustration of the vogue which still attaches to the Malachy prophecy attention may be called to the two books published on the subject by a French priest, the Abbé Joseph Maitre. The first of these, *La Prophétie des Papes attribuée à S. Malachie*, Paris, 1901, contains 880 pages. The second, *Les Papes et la Papauté d'après la Prophétie attribuée à S. Malachie*, Paris, 1902, contains 778 pages. Needless to add that the Abbé Maitre is an ardent champion of the authenticity of the prophecy.

[2] " Si bene advertimus pauca ista quae dicta sunt, *non prophetia defuit illi*, non revelatio, non ultio impiorum, non gratia sanitatum, non mutatio mentium, non denique mortuorum suscitatio " (*Vita Malachiæ*, cap. 29).

remark no word has ever been produced from any mediæval author making reference to the prophecies with which his name is now connected.[1] It was not until four centuries and a half later that the world first heard of his collection of mottoes for future Popes. In 1595 Dom Arnold Wion, a Benedictine monk, originally of Douai, published in Venice a book called *Lignum Vitæ, Ornamentum et Decus Ecclesiæ*, dealing mainly with the glories of the Benedictine Order. His work was comprehensive, and included the Cistercians as well as Benedictines proper. He had consequently occasion to mention St. Malachy, the Cistercian Archbishop of Armagh, and at the end of his short notice of the saint he remarks:

Three epistles of St. Bernard addressed to St. Malachy are still extant (viz., 313, 316, and 317). Malachy himself is reported to have been the author of some little tractates, none of which I have seen up to the present time, except a certain prophecy of his concerning the Sovereign Pontiffs. This, as it is short and has never been printed, is inserted here, seeing that many people have asked for it.

[1] J. Schmidlin has pointed out that St. Bernard in his Life of St. Malachy refers to the Archbishop's gift of prophecy in one or two other passages, but on the other hand it is certain that St. Bernard himself did not believe in a long succession of future Popes, for he always preached and maintained that the end of the world was near. We can only conclude that he knew nothing of St. Malachy's long list of 111 papal mottoes. See Schmidlin in *Festgabe Heinrich Finke gewidmet* (Münster i. W., 1904), pp. 16-17.

Then follows the list of 111 mottoes,[1] beginning with *Ex castro Tiberis*, which is assigned to Pope Celestine II (1143-4). Wion prints each motto side by side with the name of the Pope to which it refers, and with a short elucidation to explain how the phrase applied. This interpretation was, he tells us, the work of Father Alphonsus Ciacconius, O.P. Of course, when Wion gets down to his own times he can no longer offer any explanations, and so after No. 74, *De rore cœli* (From the dew of Heaven), applied to Urban VII, 1590, all the remaining mottoes are simply set down in order without comment. For our present purpose it is the early mottoes occurring before that of Urban VII which specially claim our attention. Perhaps without printing the whole list, it may be well to give a short specimen. I have selected it almost at random, and, so far as I am aware, the mottoes chosen are neither more nor less extravagant than the rest. It seems unnecessary to quote the interpretations in the original Latin.

Supposed prophecy of St. Malachy.	*Name of corresponding Pope.*	*Interpretation attributed to Ciacconius.*
(29) *Ex rosa leonina* (from a leonine rose).	Honorius IV (1285-1287).	He belonged to the family of Savelli, whose coat of arms was a rose held by two lions.

[1] *Religio depopulata*, which apparently falls to the lot of Benedict XV, is the one hundred and fourth in the series and seven still remain to be fulfilled.

Supposed prophecy of St. Malachy.	Name of corresponding Pope.	Interpretation attributed to Ciacconius.
(30) *Picus inter escas* (a magpie amongst dainties).	Nicholas IV (1288-1292)	He came from the town of *A*scoli or *E*scoli in *Pi*cenum.
(31) *Ex eremo celsus* (exalted from the desert).	Celestine V (1295).	He was formerly called Peter de Morrone,[1] and was a hermit.
(32) *Ex undararum benedictione* (from the benediction of the waves).	Boniface VIII (1294-1303).	His Christian name was Benedict, and he had waves for his coat of arms.
(33) *Concionator Patareus* (the preacher of Patara).	Benedict XI (1303-1304).	He was called Brother Nicholas,[2] and belonged to the Order of Preachers.
(34) *Defessis aquitanicis* (from the Aquitanian fesses).	Clement V (1305-1314).	He was a native of Aquitaine, and had fesses for his coat of arms.
(35) *De sutore osseo* (from the bony or osseous shoemaker).	John XXII (1316-1334).	A Frenchman, the son of a shoemaker, whose family name was Ossa.[3]

Foolish and trivial as the commentary may sound, there is no room for doubt that these interpretations and no others were intended by the author of the prophecy. The most ardent defenders of its authenticity have never suggested

---

[1] Ciacconius' interpretation, supposing it to be his, would hardly be intelligible to any one but an Italian. He apparently wishes to convey that *celsus* in the prophecy was suggested by the word *gelso*, which is a synonym in Italian for *moro*, or *morone*, a mulberry-tree. It must be remembered that in the Italian pronunciation, with a soft *g* and a soft *ch* for *c*, the words *gelso* and *celso* resemble each other more closely than they would do in English.

[2] The interpreter assumes that his readers will know that St. Nicholas was a native of Patara, and might readily be called patareus, the Patarean.

[3] This is untrue, see p. 147.

Papal Arms

anything substantially different, and once the fact is grasped that the mottoes are derived sometimes from the armorial bearings, sometimes from the cardinalitial title, sometimes from the Christian or family name, and sometimes from the place of origin of the Pope, or from a

SUPPOSED ARMS OF GREGORY X.
"Vir anguineus."

ARMS OF POPE HONORIUS IV.
"Ex rosa leonina."

combination of two or more of these elements, a sort of law will be found to run through the whole. Certainly, the identifications are in the aggregate so striking as far to transcend the possibilities of mere coincidence. It is conceivable that the motto *anguinus* (sic) *vir* (the serpentine man), assigned to Gregory X, might by mere accident have corresponded with the fact that the Pontiff in question bore a snake in his coat of arms,[1] or it might have happened by chance that Clement IV—*draco depressus* (the dragon overthrown)—displayed an eagle on his shield treading under foot a prostrate dragon;[2] but it is surely impossible that any lucky guess could show a score (or rather several score) of such hits, or could exactly fit the case of two Popes related to each other, as were the two Borgias, Callistus III and Alexander VI. I think I am right in saying that these two Popes are the only two in the list who blazoned a bull upon their escutcheon. In Malachy's list a bull is also twice mentioned, viz., in the case of just these two Popes. In the shield of Callistus III there are no quarterings, but the quadruped is represented in Panvinio with its head down, and with tufts of grass at its feet. The motto assigned to Callistus by St. Malachy is *bos pascens* (the bull grazing). In the case of Alexander the bull only appears in Panvinio in the dexter half of the shield without any indication of grass. The motto of Alexander VI in the same prophecy is *Bos Albanus in Portu* (an Alban bull in a harbour), which is explained when we remember

---

[1] These are the arms assigned him by Panvinio, but it is practically certain that they are quite incorrect. Gregory did not belong to the Visconti of Milan. See Mgr. Barbier de Montault, *Œuvres*, vol. iii., p. 366, and Woodward, *Ecclesiastical Heraldry*, p. 159.

[2] This again is wrong, as we shall see later, though given by Panvinio and those who copy him.

that Cardinal Borgia had held successively the cardinalitial titles of Episcopus Albanus and Episcopus Portuensis. No reasonable man, therefore, would hesitate to admit the preternatural character of such vaticinations, if only the fact were established that the prophecy had preceded the event. But there precisely comes the difficulty, for, as already stated, not one scrap of evidence has ever been adduced to show that St. Malachy's prophecy about the Popes had been quoted, or even heard of, before it was published by Wion in 1595.

The list of Papal prophecies in the *Lignum Vitæ*, though occupying only a few inconspicuous pages in the middle of a big book,[1] very soon attracted attention. We find it frequently reprinted in various historical works of considerable bulk, as for instance in Messingham's *Florilegium Insulæ Sanctorum*, and also issued separately as a tract of a few leaves with explanations in the vernacular.[2] In 1663 seemingly appeared the first refutation of these pretended prophecies by a Franciscan Friar named Carrière,[3] and this exposure was supported and

---

[1] *Lignum Vitæ*, pt. i, pp. 307-11. The five divisions of the work, with supplementary matter, fill more than 1800 pages in all.

[2] An edition in Latin and Dutch, printed at The Hague in 1645, is in the British Museum.

[3] This book I have not seen. Weingarten, who in his article on the subject in *Studien und Kritiken*, 1857, p. 560, gives 1629 as the date of the first edition of the *Digesta Chronologiæ Pontificiæ*, seems to have confused both title and date. See Maitre, *La Prophétie des Papes*, p. 70.

enforced by the high authority of Father Papebroech the Bollandist, and especially by Father Menestrier, another distinguished Jesuit, who devoted a special essay to the subject.[1] The arguments of these writers are in themselves conclusive. No person of sound judgment who will take the trouble to peruse the detailed analysis of the prophecies given by the last-named writer can hesitate for a moment in his verdict as to their spuriousness. He points out in the first place that there is absolutely no trace to be found of any such oracles before the appearance of Wion's book. Not only do we find no mention of them among the writings of St. Malachy's contemporaries, but no mediæval manuscript is known to contain them, no author cites them, though many interested themselves in such subjects, and Wion, who published the document with its interpretation, says not a word as to whence or under what circumstances he had obtained it.[2] Secondly, Father Menestrier lays stress upon the appearance in such a list of eight Antipopes, usually without any sign to distin-

---

[1] Lest I should seem to imply that the Society of Jesus as a body was arrayed against the authenticity of these prophecies, I may mention that the *Lux Evangelica* of Father Henry Engelgrave, S.J., took the other side, and had probably more to do with obtaining popular credence for the mottoes than any other work of that age. Father Cornelius a Lapide, in his commentary on the Apocalypse, also seems to place full confidence in the prediction.

[2] If Ciacconius, or his nephew, were really responsible for the interpretations, it is most significant that not a word is said of the prophecy in the works of this historian of the Popes.

guish them from the genuine Popes. The true Pope, Urban VI, is, on the contrary, designated by the words *de inferno prægnante* (out of the womb of hell), while the Antipope is described as *crux apostolica* (the cross of the Apostles). No doubt it might be said that the prophet looks only to the historic fact that rightly or wrongly such men did figure before the eyes of their contemporaries as Vicars of Christ; and if we were dealing with a case of clairvoyance, or second sight, the plea might be accepted. But then these are supposed to be facts communicated to the saint by divine revelation presumably for some useful end. What possible end of edification or utility can be served by a series of quibbling enigmas in which such a Pontiff as Innocent XI, a man conspicuous for his personal sanctity, is described as *bellua insatiabilis* (insatiable monster), in which another Pope is identified with the motto, to follow the received reading, of *sus in cribro* (a sow in a sieve),[1] and in which the learned and exemplary Benedict XIV figures as *animal rurale* (a country beast)?

But the most conclusive argument against the genuineness of the prophecy, as was pointed out by its earliest critics, lies in the striking contrast between the success and uniformity of the earlier

---

[1] I am tempted to think that the proper reading may be *avis*. The arms of the Crivelli, as pictured by Panvinio, show a bird (an eagle?) above the sieve. I know of no evidence that the family, as the interpreters state, ever had a sow in their coat of arms.

interpretations and the failure and wide diversity of the later ones. The document was first given to the world in 1595, and down to this epoch the mottoes without an exception[1] fit their subjects accurately. That they are far-fetched, ridiculous, and purposeless is not disputed, but, as already remarked, they follow some sort of system. After that date their interpretation becomes practically hopeless, and there is hardly a proportion of one in six in which any semblance of probability attaches to the explanations suggested. If the motto can be got to fit the subject at all, it is only by adopting a system of interpretation which is entirely without a parallel in the earlier part of the list.[2] Down to the end of the sixteenth century *there is not one single instance in which the events of any Pope's reign are alluded to in his motto.*[3] This motto refers in every case exclusively to circumstances connected with the Cardinal previously to his election to the Papacy —for instance, to his coat of arms, his family or birthplace, his episcopal sees, or title as Cardinal, his Christian name (never, be it noted,

---

[1] I believe that the slight difficulties which occur in the case of one or two, may be satisfactorily accounted for by the possible misprints or misreadings in the copy printed by Wion.

[2] Professor Harnack has been the first, I think, to lay stress upon this in the *Zeitschrift für Kirchengeschichte,* vol. iii, p. 321.

[3] Perhaps the *frumentum floccidum* of Pope Marcellus II, which seems to refer to the shortness of his reign, might be considered an exception, but, as I shall show, it is in any case an exception which proves the rule.

the name assumed by him in becoming Pope),[1] or even the manner of his early training and the Religious Order he belonged to. But of the events of the Papacy never a hint. Even such conspicuous figures as Innocent III, Boniface VIII, Nicholas V, Pius II, Leo X, are all designated by some absurd verbal quibble connected with their family name, their coats of arms, or what not, but there is absolutely not an allusion to the part each played as Head of the Church in the secular or religious history of his time.[2] On the other hand, the few Pontiffs of the last three centuries who can in any intelligible manner be connected with the mottoes assigned them, owe the identification in almost every case to the events of their Pontificate. *Peregrinus apostolicus* is no doubt an admirably appropriate label for the chequered career of Pius VI, but it describes his life as a Pope and not as a Cardinal. *Aquila rapax* may be thought by some to signalize the Pontificate of Pius VII by a reference to the ravening eagle of the first

---

[1] It may be urged that in *celsus ex eremo,* which betokens St. Celestine V, *celsus* is meant as a contraction of Celestinus ; but, as shown in a previous note, a quite different explanation is forthcoming, and this last is obviously the explanation suggested by the interpreter.

[2] Innocent III is *comes signatus,* he was a count of the family of Segni; Boniface VIII is *ex undarum benedictione,* from his Christian name Benedict, and the *waves* in his coat of arms; Nicholas V, from his humble birth at Luna, is called *de modicitate lunæ;* Pius II, who had served the two Cardinals, Capranica and Albergato, is *de capra et albergo;* Leo X, the son of *Lawrence* de Medici, and the pupil of Politian, is *de craticula Politiana,* from the gridiron of Politian.

French Empire, but again it is the Pontificate which is in question, not the Pope's antecedents before his election. *Crux de cruce* would stand well enough for the cross laid upon the shoulders of Pius IX by the white cross of Savoy, but once more the cross is one which came to him only after, and long after, he had taken up the government of the Church.

On the other hand, in the prophecies of the last three centuries an heraldic interpretation hardly ever presents itself. In the mottoes of the seventy-four Popes before 1590 there are twenty-eight plain references to different coats of arms,[1] and this in spite of the fact that the arms of many of the earlier Popes were not known. Since 1595 there have been only three mottoes which can with any sort of probability be explained by the Popes' armorial bearings. One of these instances is that of a pontiff of quite modern times. The *lumen in cœlo*, a delightfully vague description, is usually interpreted of the comet which appears with the *fleurs-de-lys* and the cypress-tree in the shield of Leo XIII. Twice before in his earlier mottoes the prophet had referred to some heavenly body, and on each occasion called it *sidus*. Why on this occasion, if he really meant a star, he should have chosen so much more ambiguous a word, does not

---

[1] L'Abbé Maitre, *La Prophétie des Papes* (Paris, 1901), pp. 194-220, considers that there are thirty-one allusions to papal coats of arms during this same period.

appear. Of the twenty-eight Popes who have reigned since 1590, no less than eleven have a single star or a group of stars displayed more or less conspicuously in their coats of arms. To each one of these the motto *lumen in cœlo* would have applied quite as well as to Leo XIII. Again, there is the motto which falls to the lot of Alexander VII; *custos montium*. His arms are three hills with a star above them, and it may be admitted that the interpretation is to this extent satisfactory. But the coincidence is far from a marvellous one. A glance at the armorial bearings of the Roman Cardinals at any period will show quite a large proportion of shields in which a group of the conventional mountain peaks looking like thimbles are conspicuously displayed. Out of the last thirty Popes, mountains appear in the arms of five. The probability against such a phrase as *montium custos* fitting any individual Pope would therefore be about six to one. But it is really much less, for if the Pontiff in question had held such a cardinalitial title as St. Martini in Montibus, St. Stephani in Monte Cœlio, or St. Petri in Monte Aureo, the prophecy would assuredly be claimed as a striking instance of successful divination. What is more, the prediction would be considered verified if such a Pope had been born, or had been bred, or had been Bishop in any one of the fifty Italian townships whose name begins with Monte, or had been Legate in Montenegro, or had lived in the Alps or the Apennines, or even had been known to take his daily constitutional on the Pincio. As for the one remaining motto which the champions of the prophecy profess to explain heraldically, I can only say that the attempt is itself a hopeless confession of weakness. On the ground that the coat of arms of Innocent XI exhibits a lion and sometimes an eagle, it is maintained that there is sufficient justification for the motto assigned to him of *bellua insatiabilis*—insatiable beast !¹

Surely it is unnecessary to argue the subject further. If the prophecy were an inspired prediction of St. Malachy in the twelfth century, it is inexplicable why the mottoes should be easily verifiable, systematic, and largely heraldic, down to the date when the prophecies were first printed, and then should suddenly change their character completely. On the supposition, however, that it is a forgery of about the year 1590, this is exactly what we should expect to find.

Of all the later mottoes, the nearest approach to a hit seems to be that which is assigned to Gregory XVI, *de balneis Etruriæ*. There *is* a place known as Bagno (Balneum) in Tuscany (*i.e.*, Etruria). It is true that Gregory was not

¹ According to Woodward, the correct blazon of the arms of Innocent XI (Odescalchi) is—" vair, on a chief gules a lion passant argent, this chief abaissé under another of the empire (eagle)." The markings of the fur vair have curiously been turned into lamps or cups in many of the copies. See *Notes and Queries*, 6th series, vol. vi, p. 82, and vol. vii, p. 198; 7th series, vol. vi, p. 205.

A Dog and a Snake   135

born there and had personally no connection with it; but he had been a Camaldolese monk, and this particular village in the Apennines, called Bagno, was associated with the life of St. Romuald, the founder of the Order, and was only a few miles from the desert of Camaldoli. Still, even here no one could ever say that the name Bagno was so intimately associated with the Camaldolese Order that it could popularly be accepted as a synonym for the desert itself. Manresa might stand for the Jesuits perhaps, and Monte Cassino for the Benedictines, but we should not dream of identifying the hermit monks of St. Romuald with the town of Bagno di Romana. As for the majority of the interpretations attached to the later prophecies by such champions of their authenticity as Maitre, Gorgeu, or Cucherat, they are hopelessly far-fetched and extravagant. For example, the motto which falls to Leo XII is *canis et coluber* (a dog and a snake). There is nothing of the sort in his coat or arms, so Cucherat is satisfied to believe that Leo combined the vigilance of a dog with the prudence of a serpent, though he suggests as equally satisfactory the explanation that the revolutionary agitators of his reign barked against him like dogs and crawled like serpents. Interpretation is easy on such terms. So again, when Urban VIII (Barberini, with three bees for his coat of arms) is designated by *lilium et rosa* (the lily and the rose), we are told that "he was a native of Florence, a town which takes its name from flowers, and the bees which appear in his coat of arms are particularly fond of lilies and roses." The rest are little better.

It must not be supposed that these considerations in any way exhaust the arguments which might be urged against the genuineness of the so-called prophecy. I reserve for later treatment one or two points which seem to me practically conclusive. But it will be best before going further to offer some explanation regarding the probable origin of the list of mottoes printed by Wion. And, be it remarked in passing, we cannot too often remind ourselves that Wion's text is the ultimate and only source of every modern copy. There is not even a single one of the mottoes which has been found existing separately and professing to derive from some other document prior to, or independent of, the *Lignum Vitæ*.

If the prophecy of St. Malachy has met with as much favour as it has done, despite all the refutations of which it has been the object, the fact, I think, is largely due to the feeling latent in many minds, that it would not have been possible or, at any rate, worth while to fabricate such a list. The tolerably minute acquaintance which it supposes with Papal history and heraldry are such that it is difficult to believe that a person so gifted—we are speaking, it must be remembered, of the year 1590—would condescend

Panvinio's Pope-Book 137

to this kind of fraud. This objection would not be without its weight if it were not that we are able to point to one, or more accurately speaking, to two definite works which offered ready to hand all the information the forger wanted. A careful examination and minute comparison of these books with the first seventy mottoes attributed to St. Malachy will render it clear beyond the possibility of doubt that the author of the prophecy worked with these books open before him. Without a single exception these volumes explain the origin of every detail, every triviality to be met with in the so-called prophecy down to the time of Paul IV (1555). The few intervening years before 1590 needed no research, they would have been fresh in the memory of every one. I speak of two works, but they were in reality but one, and they had but a single author. Onofrio Panvinio, a famous Roman antiquary, had collected, at the direct suggestion of the Sovereign Pontiff, a mass of historical material to elucidate the History of the Popes by Platina. He had compiled lists of the Cardinals created in each Pontificate, with drawings of their armorial bearings and brief summaries of the lives of those who were elected to occupy the chair of St. Peter. Somehow or other the manuscript of these supplementary collections passed out of Panvinio's keeping and apparently fell into the hands of a printer of Venice, who forthwith had all the arms engraved, and published the book in

1557 as a handsome folio volume embellished with an immense number of blocks representing the shields of Popes and Cardinals. The author got wind of this when it was too late, and bitterly complaining that the work had gone to press from a rough unfinished copy abounding in errors, he himself superintended an issue of the text of the same work, for the most part rewritten and considerably modified, which likewise saw the light at Venice in the same year, 1557. On account of the extreme haste with which the author's own edition had to be produced that it might not lag behind its rival, it was found impossible to prepare blocks with the armorial bearings. This edition therefore appeared in quarto form and without illustrations, but the text claimed to be in many ways more accurate than that of the folio copy, which was externally more sumptuous. Here then in these two works we find all the material used in fabricating the prophecies of St. Malachy. I reproduce here a specimen taken from the folio copy to illustrate the nature of the information which the forger had ready to hand as he compiled his motto for each Pontiff. Of the three shields which stand at the head the centre one is that of the Pope (Boniface VIII); the other two are those of the two earliest Cardinals of his creation. Panvinio knew nothing of the armorial bearings of the second, and according to his custom drew the shield but left it blank.

Boniface VIII 139

Below we have a concise biography of the Pope *before his election to the Papacy*. Throughout the volume no attempt is made to narrate

BONIFACIVS PP. VIII. NV. CCXVIII. AN. CHR. ∞CCXCIIII.

IN NOMINE DEI ET SALVATORIS NOSTRI
IESV CHRISTI BENEDICTI. AMEN.

ANCTISS. D. N. BONIFACIVS VIII. PONT. MAX. Benedictus natione Italus, patria Romanus ex nobili & antiqua familia Caietana Ana guia oriundus, Pontificij ciuilisque iuris peritissimus, alti cordis, & rerum humanarum experientissimus. Hic à PP. Martino IIII. Diaconus Card. in Diaconia S. Nicolai in carcere Tulliano creatus est, mox à PP. Nicolao IIII. presb. Card. est, ordinatus in tt. SS. Siluestri & Martini in montibus. Demum PP. Cœlestino V. Neapoli sponte abdicante, quùm se tantæ moli impares humeros habere cognouisset, adnitente, & iuuante Rege Carolo in eius locum omnium Cardinaliũ suffragijs in uigilia Natalis Domini, hoc est IX. Calend. Ianuarij Pontifex Maximus renunciatus est, prædecessore suo inuente. Sedit autem in sacratissima sede beati Petri Apostoli, annos octo, menses nouem, & dies decem & nouem.

the history of the Pontificate itself. The reason is very simple. The work had only been prepared, as Panvinio tells us in his preface to the quarto edition, to supplement the history of the

Popes by Platina. The detailed account of each Pontificate was to be found there, and it was useless to repeat it. The fabricator of the prophecies was content to use this *Epitome* of Panvinio in its double form to the exclusion of everything else. It placed before him the arms of the Pope, where they were known, and a few facts about his parentage, birthplace, cardinalitial titles, etc. One or two scraps extracted from this summary were woven together in a kind of oracular jargon, and behold the prophecy complete. In the case of Boniface VIII, the notice of whom is here reproduced, the forger has picked out the fact that his Christian name was Benedict, and that a wavy bend was the sole charge upon his shield, and from this he has evolved the motto already mentioned, *Ex undarum benedictione*, from the benediction of the waves. The reader will now readily see why it is that the prophecies down to the close of the sixteenth century contain no allusion to the events of any Pope's reign. They were not introduced into the mottoes, for the simple reason that they were entirely passed over in the book from which the fabricator of the mottoes was working. I have spoken of a possible exception which proves the rule. It is in the case of Pope Marcellus II, whose premature death after a few weeks' pontificate is said by Wion's interpreter (Ciacconius?) to be alluded to in the motto *Frumentum floccidum*, drooping corn.

"His arms," says the interpreter, "consisted of a stag and corn; it was *drooping* corn because he lived only a short time in the Papacy." Now as it so happens, Panvinio in his notice of Marcellus II, who was his intimate personal friend, departs rather from his usual practice, and concludes his account by a sort of little panegyric deploring the Pope's untimely death. "Whilst he strove (says Panvinio) to reform the Church of God, he sank to earth like the flower of the morning" (*tanquam flos matutinus recidit*). Is it unreasonable to suppose that this phrase taken with the wheat ears of the coat of arms suggested the *frumentum floccidum* of the prophecy?[1]

But here a champion of the Malachy prophecy will possibly raise an objection. Granted, he may say, that Panvinio supplies the materials from which a forger *might* have fabricated the first seventy mottoes, this is after all no proof that the mottoes had actually no other origin. Why could not St. Malachy have known beforehand by revelation the facts which Panvinio in his day acquired through a process of historical research?

[1] Although the arms as engraved in the folio Panvinio undoubtedly show ears of corn, it seems probable that the true blazon should be bulrushes. The family name Cervini comes from *cervo* (a stag), in Latin *cervus*. Now in Ps. xli. 1 we have Quemadmodum desiderat cervus ad fontes aquarum (As the hart panteth after the fountains of water). This suggests bulrushes, not ears of corn. See Woodward, *Ecclesiastical Heraldry*, p. 163.

To this objection it would be possible to return a very long reply, but I cannot persuade myself that an exhaustive demonstration is needed. In sum the answer amounts to this, that it is inconceivable that God could have revealed the future to one of His mediæval saints in the exact form in which the facts would afterwards be known to a renaissance scholar, with all that scholar's blunders, misapprehensions, and idiosyncrasies. Let us treat the matter as concisely as possible under these five heads.

1. Panvinio's book is a very peculiar one. As it was written to supplement Platina's Lives of the Popes, it concerns itself only with the *antecedents* of the prelates elected to the papacy, and gives no account of the history of each pontificate. Now, as we have seen, the same characteristic marks the mottoes assigned to the first seventy Popes in the Malachy list. They all find their explanation, as their interpreters admit, not in the events of each pontificate, but in those antecedent details furnished by Panvinio, *e.g.*, the Pope's family name, or coat of arms, or cardinalitial title, or birthplace, or origin. Is it not a little extraordinary that if St. Malachy, in the twelfth century, beheld a vision of the Popes to come, he should see and describe, not what each one did as Christ's Vicar, but only the title he held as cardinal, or his arms or birthplace or family connections?

2. It has always been objected against the

The Antipopes 143

prophecy that true Popes and Antipopes are placed upon the same footing. The mottoes do not, ordinarily speaking, serve to distinguish the one from the other. Strange to say, the same feature is found in Panvinio. But there are two remarkable exceptions. The Popes whom Panvinio designates Nicholas V (1327), and Clement VIII (1424), appear in his quarto edition, with the heading ANTIPAPA in large capitals, and in just these two cases, and these two cases only, we have the idea of a schism introduced into the mottoes. Nicholas V is called *Corvus schismaticus*, Clement VIII *Schisma Barchinonium*. Moreover, the order of these Popes and Antipopes, which is most peculiar, and which is censured by Menestrier and others for its historical inaccuracy, is exactly the order of the revised quarto edition of Panvinio. Probably no other book has ever been printed, save those directly founded on Panvinio, which gives the Antipopes in precisely that relative position.

3. The irrelevancies and extravagances which we note in the oracular jargon of these mottoes is over and over again explained by the casual occurrence of some word in Panvinio's brief description. For example, Nicholas III is styled "Rosa composita." The rose is in his coat of arms, but where does the *composita* come from or what does it mean? Panvinio tells us that *a morum gravitate compositus est appellatus* (folio ed., p. 177), from the seriousness of his

character he was called "the composed." So again, Nicholas V (1447, not the Antipope), who was born in Luna, is styled *De modicitate lunæ,* whatever that may be supposed to signify. The expression is only explained when we find that Panvinio describes him in the folio edition (p. 311) as *ortus modicis parentibus,* born of middle-class parents.

4. It seems an unlikely thing that if God had really made known to St. Malachy, an Irishman who lived much in France, certain distinctive characteristics which would serve to identify the future heads of His Church, He should have indicated them by phrases only comprehensible to those who have a knowledge of Italian. Alexander III's motto is *ex ansere custode* (from a guardian goose), but we can only interpret this when we learn—from Panvinio, of course, but the fact is very doubtful—that his family name was Paparo. If one happens to know that *papero* in Italian means a gosling, the connection is plain, but not otherwise. Similarly the mottoes take for granted the reader's knowledge that Caraffa is derived from *cara fe* or *fede* (Paul IV), that *gelso* and *moro* both mean mulberry-tree (Celestine V), that *albergo* means inn (Pius II), that Caccianimici means putting your enemies to flight (Eugenius IV), that Piccolomini means small man (Pius III), and so forth.

The difficulty is a serious one, for to take somewhat broader ground, if there is anything which may be regarded as a general principle in all such revelations, it is that the subjective element is never eliminated. In Holy Scripture itself the prophets show that their thought is coloured by the conditions of their daily life, and they express themselves according to the fashion and knowledge of their contemporaries. Now the pseudo-Malachy writes not as a mediæval monk, but as a post-renaissance Italian. Whatever may be said of the antiquity of the science of heraldry, it is unquestionable that its developments in the early twelfth century were of the rudest and most primitive kind.[1] The Roman of 450 years later, on the contrary, was forced to be something of a herald, for over almost every building upon which his eye rested he might distinguish the coat of arms of the Pontiff or the Prince who had erected it. It was natural enough for an idler, who found himself confronted at every turn with lilies, and mountains, and oak-trees, such as appear in the shields of the Pontiff, to amuse his fancy with mottoes like *Montium*

---

[1] The late Marquis of Bute writes: " The earliest unquestionable example of heraldry in the world is stated by Planché to be the case of Philip I, Count of Flanders, on a seal of 1164; and it is therefore rather staggering to find apparent allusions of the kind applying not only to the Pope who was reigning at that time, but to one who died in 1144. Moreover, it is certainly more probable than not that St. Malachy, who died in 1148, had never heard of any such thing as heraldry in his life."—*Dublin Review*, October, 1885, p. 380.

Custos, Fructus Jovis juvabit,[1] *Æsculapii pharmacum, Lilium et Rosa, Hyacinthus Medicorum,*[2] etc. No wonder that, as Menochius tells us in his *Stuore,* there was a superstition among the ignorant populace that the arms of every Pope until the end of the world were to be found carved somewhere upon the bronze doors of St. Peter's, and could be detected by any one, if only he had the patience to puzzle them out. But how should such thoughts come to a far-off Irish monk[3] in the destitution of the first beginnings of Clairvaux? To the late Lord Bute the mottoes seemed self-condemned by the paganism of their language. " They look," he said, " like indications of a mind so blinded by the heathenism of the later Renaissance as not to perceive their extraordinary incongruity with

---

[1] " The acorn will aid." Jove's fruit was the acorn, the fruit of his sacred tree. This was the motto of Julius II (*della Rovere*). The family name meant oak-tree, and he bore an oak-tree with golden acorns for his arms.

[2] Paul III. The *hyacinthus* stood for the Farnese lilies in his coat of arms as above. *Medicorum* came from his " title " of SS. Cosmas and Damian. Lord Bute, in his valuable essay on the Prophecy of St. Malachy (*Dublin Review,* October, 1885), sees here an allusion to the rare precious stone called the jacinth (p. 379), and thinks that it refers to an heraldic tincture.

[3] I am not urging that the mottoes cannot possibly be due to St. Malachy merely because they may seem extravagant. Some of the miracles attributed to this saint are, to use the phrase of the Abbé Vacandard, decidedly *bizarre.* The following, for instance: " Venit mulier gravida et vere gravis. Indicat se contra omnes naturæ leges retinere partum jam quindecim mensibus et diebus viginti : Compassus Malachias super novo et inaudito incommodo orat et mulier parit." (*Malachiæ Vitæ,* n. 47.)

Panvinio's Blunders

the alleged nature of the document in which they are found.'"[1]

5. But the most conclusive argument of all is the adoption and perpetuation of Panvinio's mistakes. For example, this historian, in both his editions, states that Eugenius IV had been a Celestine monk, and hence pseudo-Malachy dubs him *Lupa cœlestina*. But this is simply a blunder, as Menestrier and others have shown.[2] Eugenius was an Augustinian, not a Celestine. Again, Panvinio supposed that the father of Pope John XXII was a shoemaker named Ossa, and from this we get Malachy's motto, *De sutore osseo*, but modern research pronounces unhesitatingly that his name was Duèse or D'Euse, and entirely discredits the shoemaker story.[3] Finally, in four different cases in which the mottoes are admittedly founded on the coat of arms which the Pope in question is supposed to have borne, the motto agrees perfectly with the coat of arms figured in Panvinio, but more recent authorities declare, and with reason, that the arms so figured are quite erroneous. The four cases to which we refer are those of Alexander III, Clement IV, Gregory X, and Martin IV. In all these cases Panvinio's engraving, upon which the motto is founded, differs from the blazon given in such a modern authority as

[1] *Dublin Review*, p. 381.
[2] See for example Pastor, *History of the Popes*, Eng. trans., vol. i, p. 286, note.
[3] See Mollat, *Les Papes d'Avignon* (Paris, 1912), p. 43, note.

Woodward's *Ecclesiastical Heraldry*. It will be sufficient to consider one example here. According to pseudo-Malachy the motto belonging to Pope Clement IV (1265-69) was *draco depressus* —the dragon crushed—and this is at once explained when we look at the coat of arms provided for the Pope in Panvinio's folio edition, which shows a dragon underneath an eagle which is squeezing it in its talons. But later authorities lend no countenance to this idea. According to Woodward, Pope Clement IV's arms were: *Or, six fleurs-de-lis azure in orle;* while his family shield was *Or, an eagle displayed sable, on a bordure gules ten bezants*.[1] In either case there was no dragon, and unfortunately it was upon this feature alone that the motto of pseudo-Malachy was based.

And now before we turn to speak briefly of the possible occasion of the fabrication of these mottoes, it will be well to remind the reader of one or two points to which prominence has been given by Döllinger and others. Although no word was ever spoken of St. Malachy as a seer who concerned himself with the succession to the papacy, the famous Abbot Joachim of Flora (c. 1132-1202) was accredited with a similar series of *oracula*. He was even on this account called par excellence *papalista* or *papalarius*. The mottoes (it must be confessed, quite un-

[1] Woodward, p. 159. *Cf.* Mr. Everard Green (*Somerset Herald*) in *Notes and Queries*, 6th series, vol. vi, p. 81, and Miss Buck, *ib.*, vol. vii, p. 489.

warrantably) attributed to his authorship were not so concise as those fathered on St. Malachy, and they were much more denunciatory in tone, but they had a wonderful vogue from the early part of the fourteenth century onwards. Thus they were followed by a crowd of imitations to which such names were attached as Anselm Bishop of Marsico (probably an altogether fictitious personage), Jodochus Palmerius, the Friar Ægidius Polonus, and others. In nearly all these collections, as Döllinger points out, the same feature is observed, viz., that the early mottoes, having been composed after the event, fit their subjects at least so far that they are easily identifiable, while the later, which were really fabricated at a venture—a mere guess at what might be expected—" lose themselves more and more in meaningless, unintelligible phrases and commonplaces."[1]

Remembering, then, the prevalence of this species of composition—all of it counterfeit and much of it, as the printed editions show, still enjoying popular favour at the end of the sixteenth century and for long afterwards—we are led to ask what was the probable origin of the particular set of mottoes ascribed to St. Malachy. Two suggestions in particular have been offered to explain them. The first, which has been advocated by Hermann Weingarten,[2] lays the

[1] Döllinger, *Prophecies and the Prophetic Spirit*, p. 13.
[2] *Theologische Studien und Kritiken* (1857), pp. 555 *et seq*.

fabrication at the door of the monk who first published them, Dom Arnold Wion. The German professor points out that Wion gives absolutely no account of the document, or of how it came into his hands, and that it has never been shown to exist in any other copy than that which appeared in Wion's book. Further, we may note that this book proves the author's intimate acquaintance with the two separate editions, the Quarto and the Folio, of the *Epitome* of Panvinio, from which, as has been shown above, the list attributed to St. Malachy has almost certainly been fabricated. I may add one other item on the same side, which seems to have escaped the notice of Weingarten. The only point in which I have observed that Malachy's list contradicts the data supplied by Panvinio is in the case of Pope Clement VI. Panvinio, in both editions, calls him Bishop of Arles—*episcopus Arelatensis*—as also does Ciacconius, but Malachy's motto for him is *ex rosa Attrebatensi*—"from the rose of *Arras*." Now, in this departure from Panvinio, the pseudo-Malachy is right and Panvinio is wrong. Clement VI had been Bishop of Arras, not of Arles. It becomes a little suspicious then, when we find Wion in another place in the same book correcting Panvinio from his own personal knowledge:

This Pope [he says of Clement VI] is described by Panvinio in his Epitome in 4to as Archbishop of

Wion's Correction

Arles (Arelatensis), which I think must be a misprint for Arras (Attrebatensis); for history is silent about any such bishopric of his at Arles. On the other hand, we have just quoted what Thomas (Walsingham) says about his election to the see of Arras, and this statement is confirmed by the lists of the Bishops of Arras and the pictures of the same, which are to be seen in the Church of St. Mary at Arras, where His Holiness Clement V is represented with the insignia of the Sovereign Pontiff, as I have myself more than once seen them.[1]

None the less, I doubt if any argument can be built upon this circumstance. If Wion had the list of Malachy's supposed prophecies, and believed them to be genuine, it is extremely natural that, coming across a designation which he knew from his personal investigations to be erroneous, he should treat it simply as a blunder of the copyist, and change *Arelatensi* into *Attrebatensi* without calling attention to the substitution. As an argument, this circumstance adds nothing to the case against Wion, and I must confess that on the whole the weight of evidence seems to me against his being himself the forger.[2]

This view is also the conclusion of Prof. A. Harnack, who in an article in the *Zeitschrift für Kirchengeschichte*[3] has treated this question

---

[1] Wion, *Lignum Vitæ*, pt. i, p. 159.

[2] It is, however, to be noted that Wion was certainly very keen about prophecies. See the *Lignum Vitæ*, pt. ii, pp. 700 ff and 803 ff.

[3] Vol. iii, pp. 315 *et seq.*

with special reference to the theory of Weingarten. He points out that the aim of Wion's book was confessedly the glorification of the Benedictine Order. A man who was unscrupulous enough to fabricate a document like the so-called prophecy of St. Malachy, would certainly not have hesitated to give special prominence in the text to the Benedictine Popes, and to call attention to the fact that they had been Benedictines. Now, in this prophecy, although the Dominican Popes are noted as Dominicans, nothing shows the least Benedictine bias. Again, if Wion had fabricated the list he would surely have made it accurate up to date, and have supplied interpretations down to the time at which the list was printed and given to the world. But this is not the case. The interpretations stop with Urban VII, who died in 1590. The *Lignum Vitæ* of Wion appeared in 1595, and in the interval three Popes had succeeded—Gregory XIV, Innocent IX, Clement VIII, none of whom can be said in any way to fit their mottoes. A forger would certainly have managed better.

Professor Harnack accordingly reverts to the theory suggested long ago by F. Menestrier, the first critic who satisfactorily demolished the prophecies of pseudo-Malachy, and since then endorsed by Döllinger. He considers that the fabrication had its origin during the long *sede vacante* which preceded the election of Gregory

XIV in 1590, and that it was devised in the interest of the senior of the College of Cardinals, Cardinal Simoncelli, Bishop of Orvieto, who was plainly designated by the motto assigned to the Pope next in order—*Ex antiquitate urbis*, Orvieto being etymologically, as every man of any little education would have known, *Urbs vetus*, the old city. In support of this theory, Professor Harnack appeals strongly and forcibly to the fact pointed out above, that in the whole long list of mottoes up to that date the designations are entirely derived from circumstances of the life of each Pontiff *previous to his election*. It was the forger's object, he thinks, to show that the prophecies were always taken from something which belonged to him as Cardinal.[1]

Let me point out, however, that this argument, specious as it may appear, is not wholly convincing. The fact that the mottoes were elaborated out of Panvinio, sufficiently explains why they are confined wholly to the circumstances of each Pope's life before his election. Panvinio, as already explained, said nothing about the actual Papacy, but only of the Pope's antecedents, and the forger who used Panvinio naturally confined himself to what he found in the book before him.

[1] Görres, writing in the *Zeitschrift f. wissenschaftl. Theologie* (1903, pp. 553-62) on " Die angebliche Prophezeiung des hl. Malachias," contends that the forgery of the mottoes was a political move carried out in 1590, a time when party feeling between the Spanish and French factions in the Conclave ran very high. The arguments, however, which are adduced in support of this view seem to me quite unconvincing.

Without further discussion, then, I may content myself with indicating my own conclusion that the fabrication of the prophecy had nothing to do with the conclave of 1590, but must be assigned to the three or four last years of the life of Sixtus V. There can be no question that Simoncelli, in 1590, was an absolutely impossible candidate. We have a number of different accounts of the famous conclave which finally resulted in the election of Gregory XIV, but in no one of these that I have seen is there the slightest allusion to Simoncelli as a possible occupant of the Papal Chair. What motive could a man have for fabricating so elaborate a prophecy, which he must have known with absolute certainty would be falsified in a few weeks' time. Again, there is no mention of any party who supported the interests of Simoncelli, no hint of any ruse by which a prophecy was brought into play to influence the voting.[1] The whole struggle lay between the Spanish faction and the party identified with the policy of Sixtus V, led by his nephew, Cardinal Montalto. Even two or three years earlier, when Simoncelli was

---

[1] A considerable number of "Relations" of the events of this conclave are to be found amongst the MSS. of the British Museum. Most of these are repetitions of the account given in the *Histoire des Conclaves,* but not all. Then there is the narrative of Germonius, printed in the *Monumenta Historiæ Patriæ,* and the *Diario* of the Master of Ceremonies, Aleoni. Not one of these says a word of Simoncelli as a possible Pope, much less speaks of any prophecy being used to advance his candidature.

less old and decrepit, there was no talk of him as a likely Pope. In MS. Additional, 28,463, there is an interesting *discorso* on the chances of the various Roman Cardinals, in July, 1589, less than a year before the death of Sixtus V. Simoncelli is not even mentioned as *papabile*. Castagna, who, according to a contemporary account, was recommended to the Cardinals by Sixtus, on his death-bed,[1] and Mondovi (Laureo) are regarded as the most probable candidates. Sfondrato is also described as "running very near the Papacy." He succeeded as Gregory XIV after the short pontificate of Urban VII (Castagna), but is objected to by the author of the memorandum on the ground that he wore a perpetual smile, which many people found irritating.

If, therefore, Simoncelli was really designated by the motto *ex antiquitate urbis*, this could only have been when the possibilities of the future seemed remote and ill defined. And this appears to agree with the intrinsic probabilities of the case. It seems almost obvious that any forger who took the trouble to fabricate such a document would not be content to look only to the immediate future of the time at which he was writing, and make a guess at a single Pope, but that he would foresee the possibility of a short

---

[1] MS. Add. 21,382, fol. 140a. The same MS. contains a sonnet on the conclave held on the death of Sixtus V. All the prominent Cardinals are introduced, but not Simoncelli.

reign, or a series of short reigns, and would indicate two or three among existing Cardinals as likely to succeed in course of time, perhaps even picking out a few distinguished young men, not yet Cardinals, whom he thought likely to be raised to the purple and to become Pope some day. This is in fact what I believe to have happened in the present case. The list was perhaps fabricated about 1585, shortly after the accession of Sixtus V, and the forger—I am inclined to guess that Ciacconius himself may have fabricated it as a hoax and *jeu d'esprit*—set down the following mottoes as indicating a likely series of Pontiffs among the men he knew then living in Rome:

Motto	Persons designated.
De Rore Cœli.	Castagna (or perhaps Mondovi).
Ex antiquitate urbis.	Simoncelli (Laureo).
Pia civitas in bello.	Bellarmine (not then Cardinal).
Crux Romulea.	Santacroce.
Undosus vir.	Baronius (not then Cardinal).

Pia civitas in bello seems to me to designate *Bellarmine* in a most marked and obvious way, looking always to the principles on which the early prophecies were formed. The *Pia civitas* was Montepulciano—the shrine of a saint, the birthplace of a saintly Pontiff whose memory was still green (Pope Marcellus II, who was Bellarmine's uncle)—and itself almost proverbial for the good lives of its citizens.

Crux Romulea would fit no one so well as a

Baronius

member of the Roman family of Santa Croce. Cardinal Santa Croce, who was looked upon at the beginning of Sixtus V's reign as a most able man, died, however, in 1588. It is just possible that a nephew of his, who was then living in Rome, may have been regarded by the compiler as likely to be made Cardinal some day, and finally Pope.[1]

ARMS OF CARDINAL BARONIUS. *Undosus vir* (?).

Undosus vir, again, was Baronius, whose arms are depicted above. The pens and cross were presumably added when he became Cardinal. The waves in the family arms beneath would have suggested the *undosus*, just as the

[1] In the *Ragguaglio della Cavalcata de N. S. Gregorio XIIII* (1590), by F. Albertorio, among the *signori caporioni* "gorgeously dressed and wearing swords," is named Marcello Santacroce.

arms of Boniface VIII suggested the motto *ex undarum benedictione*.

When also we remember that *varon* or *baron* is the Spanish for man (*vir*), it is easy to understand how a Spaniard like Ciacconius might have thought that Baronius would be excellently indicated by the phrase *Undosus vir*.

Of course the point which in all this discussion most needs to be insisted on is the fact that the mottoes of pseudo-Malachy must necessarily be treated as one document. It is impossible to reject the first seventy as a barefaced imposture and to consider the thirty or forty that remain, or any part of them, as divinely inspired. The difference between the two sets is that the forger in passing from the region of the known to the future and unknown, deals more and more, as Döllinger says, "in meaningless unintelligible phrases and commonplaces." It may be worth while to copy here the whole of the remaining list from *Crux de cruce*, identified with Pius IX, down to the end. I simply print Wion's text with Lord Bute's translation:

101. Crux de cruce.   The cross from a cross.
102. Lumen in cœlo.   A light in the sky.
103. Ignis ardens.   Burning fire.
104. Religio depopulata.   Monasticism plundered (or religion laid waste).
105. Fides intrepida.   Faith undaunted.
106. Pastor angelicus.   An angelic shepherd.
107. Pastor et nauta.   A Shepherd and a sailor.
108. Flos florum.   A flower of flowers.

Mottoes still outstanding

109. De medietate lunæ. — From an half moon.
110. De labore solis. — From the toil of the sun.
111. Gloria olivæ. — The glory of the olive.

In persecutione extrema Sacræ Romanæ Ecclesiæ sedebit Petrus Romanus qui pascet oves in multis tribulationibus, quibus transactis, civitas septicollis diruetur et Judex tremendus judicabit populum.	During the last persecution of the Holy Roman Church there shall sit the Roman Peter, who shall feed the sheep amid great tribulations, and when these are passed the City of Seven Hills shall be utterly destroyed and the awful Judge will judge the people.

It is curious that these last words, if I rightly understand a remark of Wion's, do not belong to the original supposed prophecy of Malachy, but are an addition by Ciacconius. How completely Delphic in their uncertainty and consequently how much worse than useless these utterances are for any purpose of practical guidance, may be illustrated by a passage from a prophecy book, *The Christian Trumpet,* printed in England in 1875. At that date, of course, Pius IX still occupied the chair of St. Peter, and the writer remarks regarding the time to come:

According to St. Malachy, then, only ten, or at most eleven, Popes, remain to be in future more or less legitimately elected.

We say more or less legitimately elected, because out of those future Popes it is to be feared that one or two will be unlawfully elected as Antipope. It is suspected that the one designated as *Ignis ardens*

(Burning fire) shall be the first Antipope, who will be unlawfully elected in opposition to *Lumen in Cœlo* (Light in the heaven)—the legitimate successor of the present Pope. Besides some predictions announcing the deplorable event, many powerful and influential persons in Europe are at present agreed and determined to use all their efforts to elect an Antipope in order to produce a schism in the Church and to have a man who will favour their impious designs against the Catholic religion.[1]

On the other hand, the Abbé Joseph Maitre, who in two huge volumes has constituted himself the champion of the authenticity of the Malachy prophecy, holds that the motto *ignis ardens* "may either symbolize the zeal and charity of the Pontiff to be elected, or may depict the violence of the sufferings and trials he is to endure, perhaps from a terrible war, perhaps from a general conflagration or cataclysm in the moral or physical order."[2] Again, M. L'Abbé Chabauty inclines to the view that the Pope designated by *Ignis ardens* must be destined " to set on foot and carry to completion the conversion of the entire world, so that under him we shall see the realization of the promise of ' one fold and one shepherd.' " " I infer this," adds the Abbé, " not to quote other *proofs* (!), from the text, ' I have come to cast fire upon the earth and, what will I but that it be kindled.' " The

---

[1] *The Christian Trumpet* (London, 1875), p. 203.
[2] Maitre, *Les Papes et la Papanté d'après la Prophétie attribuée à St. Malachie* (Paris, 1902), p. 737.

same critic concludes that *religio depopulata* represents an anti-Pope.[1]

Could we ask for better proof of the futility of such prophecies, for all purposes of instruction or even edification, than this divergence of opinion among the most thoroughgoing defenders of the Pope-mottoes?

Lastly, I may draw attention, if only for the sake of completeness, to a development of the Malachy oracles to which publicity has been given of recent years. Here the names of the next few Popes profess to be disclosed, and the statement has been made that the text was printed in 1899. This assertion it is out of my power to verify. If it were true, it would be a remarkable fact, for the Pope corresponding to *Ignis ardens* is correctly designated as Pius X. But even if the prophet was successful in his first venture, he has come sadly to grief in his second interpretation, as he assigns to *religio depopulata* the name of Paul VI.[2] After that we can feel little interest in learning from him that Pius XI and Gregory XVII come next in order, and that the former of these after a glorious victory will become King of Italy.

[1] E. A. Chabauty, *Lettres sur les Prophéties modernes* (2nd ed., Paris, 1872), pp. 219-20.
[2] C. Niccoulaud, *Nostradamus, ses Prophéties*, Paris, 1914. M. Niccoulaud quotes for these facts *La Revue Internationale des Sociétés secrètes*, August 5th, 1913, p. 2741.

CHAPTER VII

THE FATE OF ENGLAND AND THE COMING OF ANTICHRIST

I PROPOSE to conclude these somewhat desultory chapters by speaking briefly of the two subjects in which prophets and soothsayers since mediæval times have found their principal inspiration, to wit the destiny of their own native land and the near approach of the end of the world. To discuss these themes in any great detail does not seem needful; for here, more than anywhere else, all verification being indefinitely remote, extravagance and incoherence are particularly likely to prevail. But it would argue a certain incompleteness in this survey of modern prophetic books, if these topics which are apt to occupy so much space in their pages were passed over entirely without comment.

For the past history of " national prophecies," as they have been called, I can only advise the reader to consult the third chapter of Döllinger's essay. The subject is too extensive to admit of my summarizing it here. Neither will space allow us to busy ourselves with foreign countries and with the beliefs regarding the future which in their case have often grown out of deeply-rooted popular traditions. Of this species of folklore little probably now survives in England; although in the sister Isle, Professor O'Curry, half a century ago, wrote pathetically of the prevalence of such predictions.

"I have myself known," he said, "hundreds of people, some highly educated men and women amongst them, who have often neglected to attend to their worldly advancement, in expectation that the false promises of these so-called prophecies—many of them gross forgeries of our own day—would in some never accurately specified time bring about such changes in the state of the country as must restore it to its ancient condition. And the believers in these idle dreams were but too sure to sit down and wait for the coming of the golden age; as if it were fated to overtake them without the slightest effort of their own to attain happiness or independence.'"[1]

In England, as just remarked, there has been comparatively little of this, especially in recent times, but as the British Empire plays a part of some importance in the drama of the world, any dearth of native prophets has been compensated for by the interest which the seers of other countries have taken in the destinies of perfidious Albion.

Something has already been said of one or two prognostics of the French astrologer

[1] Eugene O'Curry, *Lectures on the Manuscript Materials of Ancient Irish History* (Dublin, 1878), p. 431.

Nostradamus regarding London in the seventeenth century, and, indeed, there are many others, hardly less curious, which might have been cited from the same source. But I will content myself now with reproducing one other quatrain which, in view of the fact that it was printed a good twenty years before the defeat of the Spanish Armada, must certainly be counted a remarkable utterance. The words of Nostradamus are these:

Le grand Empire sera par l'Angleterre
Le Pempotam[1] des ans plus de trois cens,
Grandes copies passer par mer et terre;
Les Lusitains n'en seront pas contens.[2]

A seventeenth century English version translated it thus:

England of Empire shall be long the seat,
More than three hundred years continuing great.
Large forces thence shall pass through lands and seas
To the disquiet of the Portuguese.

Is this to be understood as a prophecy of the maritime dominion of England? Portugal certainly was the great naval power in the East Indies at the time when this was written, and it was the Portuguese rather than the Spaniards that England was destined to supplant. At the same time it is very doubtful whether we have anything more here than a masterpiece of

---

[1] A dreadful hybrid word which seems to be derived from τᾶν potens = all powerful.
[2] *Century*, x, 100.

Rule Britannia Foreshadowed

Delphic ambiguity. Sea power, after all, is not directly mentioned. Moreover, if it had chanced that France had conquered England, and by means of that conquest (*par l'Angleterre*) had acquired an overseas empire, the prognostic would have seemed to be even more strikingly fulfilled than it is now. Undoubtedly the unrivalled success of Nostradamus's oracles is due to the fact that avoiding all orderly arrangement either chronological or topographical, and refraining almost entirely from categoric statements, it is impossible ever to say that a particular prognostic has missed its mark, while amongst the multitude of political occurrences vaguely outlined, some quite startling coincidences are sure to be observed in the course of years. In other words, Nostradamus provides an ingenious system of divination in which the misses can never be recorded and only the hits come to the surface. For the reputation of the would-be prophet such conditions are naturally ideal.

Except for the implied limitation of England's maritime dominion to 300 years, this prognostic of Nostradamus is distinctly favourable. Other foreign prophécies regarding the destiny of Britain are not so encouraging. For example, the Père Nectou, who had been a Jesuit and Provincial of Aquitaine before the suppression of the Society, was supposed to have made many remarkable prophecies towards the close of the eighteenth century. Some of these, referring to individuals, are said to have been fulfilled in a most surprising way. In dealing with public events he does not seem to have been so successful; at any rate, fulfilment has so far been delayed. Thus we are told that he predicted a second revolution in his native country, adding that:

During this revolution, which will very likely be general and not confined to France, Paris will be destroyed so completely that twenty years afterwards fathers, walking over its ruins with their children, the children will inquire what place that was. To whom they will answer: "My child, this was formerly a great city which God has destroyed on account of its crimes."[1]

It may be, however, that the appointed hour has not yet arrived, for the Père Nectou went on: " As when the fig-tree begins to sprout and produces leaves, it is a certain sign that the summer is near, so when England shall begin to wane in power, the destruction of Paris will be near at hand."

This shall be as a sign. England shall, in her turn, experience a more frightful revolution than that of France. It shall continue so long as to give time to France to recover her strength, and then she will help England to return to order and peace.[2]

The Revolution which is to be the downfall of England's greatness has long been a rather

[1] *Voix Prophétiques*, 5th ed., vol. ii, p. 239.
[2] *Ib.*, p. 249.

Mlle. Couédon

favourite theme with the seers of the Continent, particularly in Germany. For example, here is a summary estimate of the fate of England found in a Catholic work, already referred to, printed thirty or forty years back, and known as *Das Buch der Wahr—und Weissagungen.* It has gone through more than one edition.

England has caused much mischief in Germany and other countries, and has put upon them many an insult. She will continue through intrigues and bribery of all kinds to frustrate all efforts at reformation. Ireland will rise in revolt and come victoriously out of the contest. England's star is on the wane, and it is only by perpetual trickery that this nation of shopkeepers is preserved for a short time from utter ruin.

The edition from which I quote this was printed in 1884.[1]

Again a certain Mlle. Couédon, who was much consulted as an oracle in Paris, found herself inspired, at the time of Queen Victoria's second Jubilee, to deliver some most startling prophecies regarding the future of Great Britain. She announced, amongst other things, the restoration of the Stuarts:

> L'Angleterre sera changée
> Je la vois démembrée;
> Une famille qui a regné
> Et qu'on a empêchée,

---

[1] *Das Buch der Wahr—und Weissagungen* (Regensburg, 1884), Appendix.

> Je la vois remonter ;
> Un roi du passé,
> Lui sera donné,
> Quand ceux, qui ont usurpé
> Seront détrônés.[1]

Still more alarming were the calamities which Mlle. Couédon predicted as threatening England's naval supremacy:

> Quant au jubilé
> Pour cette Reine il faut prier,
> Les Anglais vont changer,
> Les Indes leur seront ôtées.
> Je vois la guerre déclarée.
> Je vois leur flotte décimée,
> Je la vois submergée ;
> Il n'en va pas rester.

If anyone were disposed to take these oracles at all seriously, he might find consolation in the fact that while Mlle. Couédon declared that a vast European conflict would break out in the immediate future, she also predicted that France would have to support the struggle alone. Russia, on which her hopes had been built, would not stir a finger to help her.

> Ce que vous avez rêvé
> Il n'y faut pas compter.

---

[1] *L'Echo du Merveilleux*, February 1st, 1897: "England will be changed; I see her dismembered; a family which reigned before and which has been attainted, I see it restored. A king of a former dynasty will be given to her, when those who usurped their power will be dethroned."

Also that Paris would be burnt to the ground, and that without delay.

> Le feu va y passer
> Et cela sans tarder.[1]

Despite these gloomy forebodings there have been not a few among those who believed themselves prophetically inspired who have written concerning England with great sympathy. The most famous of these was the mystic Bartholomew Holzhauser in the time of the early Stuarts.

This venerable servant of God, who was born of humble parents in 1613 not far from Augsburg, was the founder of an Institute of Secular Priests, which met with considerable favour in his native country. He was a man of remarkable piety, and was held by many of his contemporaries to be possessed of extraordinary prophetic gifts. Certain visions of his were written down by him and collected into one manuscript volume towards the beginning of the year 1646. In these, it appears, he asserted that England would fall into extreme misery, that the King would be slain, and that afterwards the Kingdom of England would return to the ancient

---

[1] *L'Echo du Merveilleux,* July 1st, 1897 : " As for the Jubilee, we must pray for the poor Queen ; a change is to come over England. The Indies will be taken from them ; I see war declared ; I see their fleet decimated ; I see it sunk ; nothing will be left of it." *Cf.* Marquis de Guiry, *Mlle. Couédon est elle inspirée de Dieu?* (Paris, 1899)—a question which the author answers in the affirmative !

Roman faith, and the English achieve more for the Church than on their first conversion to Christianity. Among the friends of Holzhauser was a Jesuit, Father Lyprand, who after his death described how he had met him during one of his visits to Ingolstadt, and as a report had been for some time current that Charles I of England, who was then still living, was likely to become a Catholic, Father Lyprand asked the mystic how this could be reconciled with his prophecy about England. On this Holzhauser replied in a very confident manner: " King Charles of England is neither now a Catholic, nor will he ever become a Catholic." " The event," says Father Lyprand, " proved the truth of his words. At the same time he informed me that he knew from God that the Swede would never have a footing in the German Empire, and that the Rhine would return to its ancient master."

As to Bartholomew's prophecies in general, Father Lyprand expresses himself with caution. "I have always been of opinion," he wrote, "that he went to work without any guile, and that his natural parts were inadequate to their fabrication . . . but although I hold it as probable enough, nay, as extremely probable, that Holzhauser had received from God the gift of prophecy, yet I would not venture to assert that he always rightly understood the prophecies communicated to him; for it is agreed among theologians that the first gift may exist without the second.'"

It appears that during the period of the travels, Holzhauser was presented to him at Geisenheim, and told him something of his visions, recommending to His Majesty's protection the Catholic religion in England and the priests who were labouring there. The King, it is stated, gave him his hand and promised to be mindful of his request; and here Holzhauser's biographer remarks:

It is astonishing with what a burning zeal Holzhauser laboured to bring about the conversion of England. This was the marrow of his thoughts—the subject of his conversation—the sum of all his desires. With his blood he would fain have washed away, had he been permitted, all the errors of heresy. No resolution was so fixedly implanted in him, as to go to England, and there, utterly regardless of any risk he might run for his life, make a beginning towards a restoration of the Catholic faith. He awaited only the Elector's permission to prosecute this voyage. This permission he would have sought with earnest prayers had he not been overcome by the still more urgent solicitations of his friends, Gündel and Vogt, and been induced to defer for one or several years the execution of a project, which he never would entirely give up, in order, in the first place, to consolidate his rising Institute until such time as his presence might be more easily dispensed

[1] Gaduel, *Vie de Barthélemy Holzhauser* (Paris, 1861), p. 369. The letter of Father Lyprand was written in 1660. The text is in J. D. Gruber, *Prodromus*, pp. 792-8.

with. It was with difficulty he could be held back from this project.[1]

Perhaps the most remarkable passage in his visions bearing on England is the following:

I stood in the year 1635 by the Danube, giving alms to the banished, and offering up prayers for the whole earth. I stood towards the north and the west, and my heart poured itself out in many lamentations before God, saying: "How long will the adversary hold this kingdom in bondage, which swimmeth with the blood of martyrs, spilled by that accursed woman Jezebel, as she wished to reign in the Church of God?" And I heard at the same time that the lawful sacrifice would be intermitted for one hundred and twenty years; and on the other side of the sea I saw immense lands, and how peoples and tongues thronged together, and how the land was inwardly shaken by armies, as by an earthquake. The prodigious multitude I saw divided, and I beheld the king standing in the midst. And it was told me, "All rests with the king, and the king is, as it were, sold."

And towards the west the heavens were opened, and the land trembled as with an earthquake, and the nations were shaken, and terror came over the whole kingdom; and it was told me: "On the king dependeth the salvation of the people!" And it seemed to me as if he refused; and I heard: "If the king will not, then will he be smitten." And the heavens again opened towards the west; a large, fiery ball came down, flew oblique, and smote the king. And now his kingdom rested in peace, and the land was illuminated.

[1] L. Clarus, *Bartholomæus Holzhauser; Lebensgeschichte*, p. 69.

And lo! I saw a ship sailing on the sea, and arrive in port, and righteous and holy men, who were in the ship, landed, and they began to preach the Gospel in those countries. They prospered in their undertaking; and that land returned to peace and to the sanctification of Jesus Christ.[1]

That the Holy Sacrifice should be intermitted for 120 years does not seem to me, as it apparently seemed to the writer of the article in the *Dublin Review*, from which I quote it, a remarkably happy hit. In one quite true sense, that of actual fact, the offering up of the Mass was never interrupted in England. If, on the other hand, we take account of the period of the legal prohibition, the penal statutes which rendered the saying of Mass a criminal offence, were in force for within a few years of two centuries. Neither has the "landing of holy men" in England—by which we are no doubt meant to understand the clergy of France exiled at the Revolution, together with the younger religious Orders, such as the Passionists and the Redemptorists—brought us perceptibly nearer the conversion of the nation as a whole. But amid the enthusiasm of the Oxford movement and the restoration of the Catholic hierarchy, there must have been many to whom the return of England to the faith seemed very near. It was this expectation which no doubt led some amongst them to attach a new meaning to the prophecy

[1] Translated in the *Dublin Review*, September, 1850, p. 133.

of St. Edward the Confessor. That monarch a few hours before he passed away was supernaturally visited, as he believed, by two holy monks whom he had known in his youth. Appearing to him in a vision, they denounced the grievous corruptions of the Church and State, and warned him that on this account God had laid a curse upon the realm of England. The King, after vainly enquiring whether this sentence could in any way be averted, finally asked how long the curse should last. To which they replied :

In that day when a green tree shall be cut away from the midst of its trunk, when it shall be carried away for the space of three furlongs from its root, when without the help of man it shall join itself again to its trunk and shall again put forth leaves and bear fruit in its season—then first shall be the time when the woes of England shall come to an end.[1]

Contemporary evidence makes it practically certain that St. Edward on his death-bed did narrate some such vision to those who stood round; and in the twelfth century Englishmen commonly interpreted the prophecy as foreshadowing the restoration of the old Saxon line by the marriage of Henry I with Eadgyth or Matilda, after continuity had been broken for three generations by the intrusion of the usurpers Harold, William the Conqueror, and William Rufus. But the enthusiasts of the

[1] Freeman, *Norman Conquest,* vol. iii, p. 11.

"Second Spring" attached quite a different meaning to the prediction. The curse in their opinion was to last not for three reigns, but for three centuries, during which the Church of England, by the act of Henry VIII and his daughter Elizabeth, should be severed from the true vine, the parent trunk of Rome. Only then would the curse be removed when, without the help of man, the bough should again be united to its root through the submission of England to the Holy See.

Turning now to the anticipation of the coming of Antichrist and the end of the world, there can be no doubt that this topic, remaining substantially the same under an infinite variety of forms, has attracted the deep interest of Christians since the time of the Apostles. It is not my intention here to discuss the matter historically or to attempt to disentangle the extremely complicated story of the Antichrist legend. The investigation has been carried out very systematically by such scholars as Zezschwitz, Bousset, R. H. Charles, and others. Let it be sufficient to recognize the fact that some elements of the myth go back to pre-Christian times, while others are derived from the canonical scriptures (notably from the Epistles of St. Paul to the Thessalonians, the First Epistle of St. John, and the Apocalypse), and others again from the Apocrypha of the New Testament. Among these last we may reckon the document commonly known as the *Ascension of Isaiah,* which Dr. Charles considers can be analysed into three more primitive components, one of them being what he calls " the Testament of Hezekiah," and dating, as he believes, from the actual time of the Apostles ("between 88 and 100 A.D.").[1] Whatever view we may hold of the genesis of the *Ascension,* the passage concerning the near approach of the end of the world is of remarkable interest. Here an Antichrist is introduced, though he is not called by that name, who is really Satan incarnate, clothed in the likeness of the Emperor Nero, " the slayer of his mother," into whose hands also the Apostle St. Peter was delivered.[2] The name Beliar (= the Belial of 2 Cor. vi. 15) is used simply as a personal name for Satan-Antichrist.

The prominence here given to the Emperor Nero as a sort of type of Antichrist is in full accord with the most probable interpretation of the verse of the Apocalypse concerning the number of the beast. "He that hath understanding let him count the number of the beast. For it is the number of a man : and the number of him is six hundred and sixty and six" (Apoc. xiii. 18). Now the words NERO CÆSAR, written in Aramaic, contain letters, the numerical values of which amount to 666, and what is even

---

[1] Professor Burkitt in his Schweich lecture on *Jewish and Christian Apocalypses,* p. 45, protests against this dissection.

[2] It seems that at this very early date St. Paul had not yet commonly come to be counted among the twelve Apostles.

more significant, another spelling of the same words would yield the total 616, which happens to be a variant reading found in some early manuscripts of the Apocalypse. It is also certain from such early Christian documents as the Epistle of Barnabas that considerable attention was paid to the numerical equivalent of the letters of proper names. Also it may be noticed that the whole extract from the *Ascension of Isaiah* is very similar in spirit to the Gog and Magog passage in the Apocalypse (xx. 7-10), while the duration of the rule of Beliar is, no doubt, suggested by Dan. vii. 25, and xii. 11.

And now Hezekiah and Josab, my son, these are the days of the completion of the world. After it is consummated, Beliar, the great ruler, the king of this world, will descend, who hath ruled it since it came into being; yea, he will descend from his firmament in the likeness of a man, a lawless king, the slayer of his mother, who himself will persecute the plant which the twelve Apostles of the Beloved have planted. Of the twelve, one (*i.e.*, St. Peter) will be delivered into his hands. This ruler in the form of that king will come, and there will come with him all the powers of this world, and they will hearken unto him in all that he desires. And at his word the sun will rise at night and he will make the moon to appear at the sixth hour. And all that he hath desired he will do in the world. He will do and speak like the Beloved and he will say: " I am God, and before me there has been none." And all the people in the world will believe in him, and they will sacrifice to him and they will serve him, saying: "This is God, and beside him there is no other." And the greater number of those who shall have been associated together in order to receive the Beloved he will turn aside after him. And there will be the power of miracles in every city and region, and he will set up his image before him in every city. And he shall bear sway three years and seven months and twenty-seven days. And many believers and saints having seen Him for whom they were hoping, who was crucified, Jesus the Lord Christ, and those also who were believers in Him—of these a few in those days will be left as His servants, while they flee from desert to desert, awaiting the coming of the Beloved. And after one thousand three hundred and thirty-two days the Lord will come with His angels and with the armies of the holy ones from the seventh heaven, and He will drag Beliar into Gehenna and also his armies. And He will give rest to the godly whom He shall find in the body in this world and to all who because of their faith have execrated Beliar and his kings.[1]

Passing from Apostolic times to the early Middle Ages, we find that the approach of the end of the world was still an absorbing topic of interest, though men's ideas now centred very largely upon the anticipated peaceful reign of a world-ruling earthly monarch, who was to reduce all Christendom to harmony, and the contumacious having been previously exterminated, to convert Jews, Turks, and Pagans to the acceptance of the law of the Gospel. It was

---

[1] Charles, *The Ascension of Isaiah*, pp. 24-34.

Adso's Frankish Emperor

only after this preliminary period of peace and happiness, a sort of renewal of the golden age, that Antichrist would be permitted to devastate and seduce mankind, while he in turn, after his brief three years of desolating tyranny, would be cast down from his throne by St. Michael and the angels of God, who would at the same time destroy the world and all its inhabitants to usher in the day of general judgment. Perhaps the most primitive and fundamental presentment of this conception, so popular in the Carolingian epoch, was that contained in the letter of the monk Adso, sent in A.D. 954 to Queen Gerberga, wife of Louis IV (Louis d'Outremer). The most significant passage in the document is the following:

This is why the Apostle Paul says that Antichrist will not come into the world until rebellion has gone before—that is to say, until all the kingdoms which were at first subject to the Roman Empire have thrown off the yoke.

Now this time has not yet come; for although we see the Roman Empire in great part overthrown, still as long as the kings of the Franks shall last, who are destined to maintain the Empire of Rome, the dignity of the Roman Empire shall not be utterly destroyed, because it will survive in these kings.

Indeed, some of our teachers even say that a king of the Franks will possess the entire Roman Empire. This king will be the greatest and the last of all monarchs. And after having prosperously governed his kingdom he will come in the end to Jerusalem, and he will lay down his sceptre and his crown upon the Mount of Olives. This will be the end and consummation of the Empire of Rome and of Christendom. And the same doctors add that immediately afterwards, according to the before-mentioned text of the Apostle Paul, the Antichrist will come.[1]

It was natural that with the anticipation of this all-conquering and most religious monarch there should in time come to be associated the conception of a Saintly Pope, who would be the ideal of rulers in the spiritual order, as the great king of Frankish race was destined to be the ideal of temporal sovereigns. Whether the Abbot Joachim, of Flora, was really the author of this attractive vision of a "Papa Angelicus," as was afterwards commonly believed, seems more than doubtful, but the dream undoubtedly belongs to the century of Joachim's death. In the *Opus Tertium,* addressed by the famous English Franciscan, Roger Bacon, to Pope Clement IV in 1267, occurs the following passage:

For forty years past it has been prophesied, and many in visions have seen the same, that there will be one Pope in these our days (*his temporibus*), who will purge the canon law and the Church of God of the quibbles and the knavery of the lawyers, and that justice will be done universally without contentious litigation. And on account of the holiness, the uprightness, and the justice of this Pope it will come to pass that the Greeks will return to the obedience of

---

[1] Sackur, *Sibyllinische Texte und Forschungen—Pseudo-Methodius,* etc. (Halle, 1898), p. 110.

the Roman Church, and that in great part the Tartars will be converted to the faith and the Saracens will be destroyed; and so " there shall be one fold and one shepherd," to quote the word which the prophet had ringing in his ears. And one who saw these things in revelation said and still maintains that he himself will see all these marvels come to pass in his own lifetime.[1]

Roger Bacon had also clearly heard that the reformation of the Church was to be accomplished by a great Pope and a great King working in conjunction, and that the end of the world was probably near at hand;[2] still he does not himself assert this. Great preachers like St. Vincent Ferrer and Savonarola in the fifteenth century were much more explicit in their pronouncements. St. Vincent in particular for several years together preached throughout France and Spain, as a matter, not of opinion, but of certain knowledge, that the coming of Antichrist was imminent. Being denounced on this account to Benedict XIII the Pope of his obedience (it was during the period of the great schism) St. Vincent justified himself to the Pontiff in a long and reasoned statement, in which he declared that " the time of Antichrist and the end of the world will be soon, and very soon, and in exceeding short space " (*cito et*

---

[1] F. Rogeri Bacon, *Opera Inedita*, ed. J. S. Brewer (Rolls Series), p. 86.
[2] *Ib.*, pp. 403-4.

bene cito et valde breviter). He added that he was himself convinced that Antichrist had already been born some time before, and he justifies this belief by certain miraculous experiences of his own, as well as by the testimony of others and by the evidence of the demons whom he had questioned when exorcising possessed persons. To use his own words:

> From all these facts there has been formed in my mind an opinion and a probable belief, though not such as I can proclaim for absolute certainty, that Antichrist has already been born these nine years past. But as for the conviction which I have already stated,[1] to wit, that soon, quite soon and very shortly, the time of Antichrist and the end of the world will be upon us, I proclaim it everywhere with certainty and without misgiving, "the Lord working with me and confirming the word by the signs that follow."[2]

Further, St. Vincent both said in his sermons and told the Pope that he (Vincent) himself was the angel spoken of in the Apocalypse (xiv. 6-7), who was sent to proclaim with a great voice: "Fear God and give Him glory for the hour of His judgment is come."[3]

He stated also that when he announced that

---

[1] He had previously written, "Quarta conclusio est quod tempus Antichristi et finis mundi erunt cito et bene cito et valde breviter." F. Fagès, O.P., *Notes et Documents de l'Histoire de St. Vincent Ferrier* (Paris, 1905), p. 220.

[2] Fagès, *Notes et Documents*, p. 223.

[3] Fagès, *Histoire de St. Vincent Ferrier* (Paris, 1901), vol. i, pp. 312 *et seq.*

the end of the world would come soon, he meant this in the proper sense of the words (*proprie et stricte loquendo*), while contemporaries declared that he worked the stupendous miracle of recalling a dead person to life to witness the truth of what he prophesied.

But although all this happened more than five hundred years ago the end of the world has not yet arrived. So again we learn from no less a person than St. Bernard of Clairvaux that St. Norbert, the founder of the Premonstratensians, prophesied about the year 1128 that the coming of Antichrist might be expected immediately. " I asked him," writes St. Bernard, " what were his ideas about Antichrist. He declared that he knew in a very certain way that he would be manifested in this generation (*ea quae nunc est generatione revelandum illum esse*). As I did not share his belief, I asked him his reasons, but his reply did not satisfy me."¹ St. Francis of Paolo, on the other hand, the founder of the Minims, in a most astounding series of letters to a Neapolitan nobleman, predicted that before the expiration of 400 years (he was writing in 1485) a descendant of his should institute the last and greatest of all the religious orders, a military order of " Cross bearers," who would exterminate all the Mohammedans and unbelievers left unconverted in the last age of the world. If we could put any confidence in the

¹ St. Bernard, Ep. 56; Migne, P.L., clxxxi, 162.

authenticity of these letters,[1] the Saint wrote to his correspondent in such terms as these:

God Almighty will exalt a very poor man of the blood of the Emperor Constantine, son of St. Helena, and of the seed of Pepin, who shall on his breast wear the sign which you have seen at the beginning of this letter (+). Through the power of the Most High he shall confound the tyrants, the heretics, and infidels. He will gather a grand army, and the angels shall fight for them; they shall kill all God's enemies. O my Lord! that man shall be one of your posterity, because you come from the blood of Pepin.

Or again in another of the letters:

My Excellent Lord,—Let your soul rejoice! for his Divine Majesty manifests through you such wonderful signs and great miracles, according to what I, by God's will, have often and again written and foretold to you. One of your posterity shall achieve greater deeds and work greater wonders than your lordship. That man will be a great sinner in his youth, but like St. Paul he shall be drawn and converted to God. He shall be the great founder of a new religious order different from all the others. He shall divide it into three classes, namely: 1. Military knights; 2. Solitary priests; 3. Most pious hospitallers. This shall be the last religious order in the Church, and it will do more good for our holy religion than all other religious institutes. By force of arms he shall take possession of a great kingdom. He shall destroy the sect of Mahomet, extirpate all

---

[1] The letters are printed in Spanish by Montoya, the historiographer of the Minims, as an appendix to his *Coronica General de la Orden de los Minimos*, Madrid, 1619.

tyrants and heresies. He shall bring the world to a holy mode of life. There will be one fold and one Shepherd. He shall reign until the end of time. On the whole earth there shall be only twelve kings, one emperor, and one pope. Rich gentlemen shall be very few, but all saints. May Jesus Christ be praised and blessed; for he has vouchsafed to grant to me, a poor unworthy sinner, the spirit of prophecy, not in an obscure way as to His other servants, but has enabled me to write and to speak in a most clear manner.

That these letters were authentic I cannot for a moment believe, but they were accepted by Montoya and by such scholars as Morales, Cornelius a Lapide, and a number of others, and they therefore reflect not unfairly the tone of mind which in the seventeenth century prevailed among religious people even with some pretence to learning. It is not surprising, then, to find that such a mystic as Holzhauser, when interpreting the Apocalypse, speaks with confidence of the long-hoped-for epoch of universal reconciliation.

Like most of the prophets who committed themselves in any detail to a picture of the last age of the world, Holzhauser calls up a wonderful vision of the peace and happiness that will prevail before the coming of Antichrist. This belief may be traced back to the *Papa Angelicus* of Abbot Joachim or Bacon, and in nearly all these prognostics the ecclesiastical and civil powers are represented as acting in perfect accord. Thus the German mystic writes:

> The sixth period of the Church—the *status consolationis*—begins with the Holy Pope and the Powerful Emperor, and terminates with the birth of Antichrist.
>
> This will be an age of solace, wherein God will console His Church after the many mortifications and afflictions she had endured in the fifth period. *For all nations will be brought to the unity of the true Catholic faith.*
>
> A type of this period was the sixth age of the old world, from the deliverance of the Israelites out of the Babylonish captivity, and the rebuilding of the city and of the temple of Jerusalem, down to the coming of Christ. As God gladdened His people by the rebuilding of the temple and of the holy city; as all kingdoms and nations were subjected to the Roman Empire; and Cæsar Augustus, the most powerful and excellent monarch, after vanquishing all his enemies, gave for fifty-six years peace to the world: so will God pour out upon His Church, that witnessed in the fifth period nought but affliction, the most abundant consolations. But this happy age will be ushered in under the following circumstances. When all is desolated with war; when the Church and the priests must pay taxes; when Catholics are oppressed by heretics and their faithless fellow-religionists; when monarchs are murdered; subjects oppressed; when riches are extirpated; when everything concurs to bring about the establishment of republics, then will the hand of the Almighty produce a marvellous change, according to human notions seemingly impossible. For that strong monarch (whose name is

to be the *help of God*), will as the envoy of the Almighty, root up these republics. He will subject all things to himself, and will zealously assist the true Church of Christ. All heresies will be banished into hell; the Turkish Empire will be overthrown to its foundations, and his dominion will extend from east to west. All nations will come, and will worship the Lord in the one true Catholic faith. Many righteous men will flourish, and many learned men will arise. Men will love justice and righteousness, and peace will dwell on the whole earth. For the Omnipotent will bind Satan for many years until the advent of him who is to come—the son of perdition.

In respect to perfection, this period corresponds to the sixth day of creation, on which God created man after His own image, and subjected to him, as lord of creation, all creatures of the earth. So will man be now a true image of God (in righteousness and holiness), and the strong monarch will rule over all nations.

The sixth gift of the Spirit, the fear of the Lord, will in this period be poured out upon the Church; for men will fear the Lord their God, keep His commandments, and serve Him with their whole heart. The Scriptures will be understood after one uniform fashion, without contradiction and error, so that all will marvel they had so long misunderstood the clear sense of Holy Writ. The sciences will be multiplied and completed, and men will receive extraordinary illumination in natural, as well as divine knowledge.[1]

If this teaching is to be generally accepted, and it has prevailed as the more common opinion for

---

[1] Beykirch, pp. 27-9.

many centuries, the immediate coming of Antichrist is not yet to be feared, for most assuredly that age of grace which is to precede his advent is still far off.

At the same time among the multitude of writers, both ancient and modern, who have treated of Antichrist and the end of the world, the greatest diversity of view prevails, not only with regard to the time of the second coming of the Son of man, but also with regard to the character and order of those occurrences which are to herald His approach. The quaint legend prevalent in the later Middle Ages, which recounted the whole history of Antichrist from his portentous birth to his destruction at Jerusalem, together with the marvellous preaching of Enoch and Elias (identified with the two " witnesses " of Apoc. xi. 3-12), is not now, of course, accepted with the same unquestioning faith as formerly; but the belief in a personal Antichrist seems still to be general amongst those who incline to a conservative interpretation of Holy Scripture.[1] The late Cardinal Newman pointed out long ago in his essay on " The Patristical Idea of Antichrist," published as one of the *Tracts for the Times* in 1838, that it was the universal tradition of the early Church " that Antichrist is one individual man, not a power—not a mere ethical

---

[1] The Abbé A. Chauffard, for example, published several books in 1893 and 1894 dealing with the coming of Antichrist, the best known of which perhaps is *La Révélation de S. Jean et le prochain grand règne de l'Eglise,* Paris, 1894. On the other

spirit or a political system, not a dynasty or succession of rulers "; and in reprinting this essay in 1872, he added nothing to indicate that his views on this matter had undergone any change. The question cannot be discussed here, but it may be noted that, as in the days of St. Vincent Ferrer, so of recent years the belief in the near coming of a personal Antichrist has led, especially at times of religious unrest, to many extravagances of superstition and credulity. It will be remembered that the most objectionable features of the Diana Vaughan myth were cunningly devised by Leo Taxil to trade on this common expectation of pious Catholics. But even among those who regard the Apocalypse as an entirely prophetic document, there still remains the widest divergence of view with regard to its chronology, and it may be noted that a learned Dominican, Père Gallois, writing some years ago in the *Revue Biblique*,[1] not only argues in favour of a modified Millenarianism, but supposes that this thousand years of peace in the Church is to follow, not to precede, the period of Antichrist's dominion. In all this confusion and conflict of opinion the only thing upon which we can lay hand, I may note that Colonel J. L. Ratton, who, after two previous apocalyptic works, published in 1912 a book called *The Apocalypse of St. John*, which is dedicated to Cardinal Bourne, deprecates the idea of " an anthropomorphic Antichrist," remarking that " Antichrist is a movement, not a man " (p. 252).

[1] See the *Revue Biblique*, 1893, pp. 384-430 and 506-43; 1894, pp. 357-74.

stress with any sense of security is that utterance of our Saviour, the very language of which conveys so marked an emphasis: "But of that day or hour no man knoweth, neither the angels in heaven, nor the Son, but (only) the Father" (Mark xiii. 32).

THE END.

CPSIA information can be obtained at www.ICGtesting.com
Printed in the USA
LVOW10s1911190114

370045LV00024B/1237/P